MOTORCYCLES AND MEMORIES

ADVENTURE BEYOND THE ROAD

ERIC D. BEAL

LAST BASTION MEDIA

———————————

For permission requests, contact the author at:

Last Bastion Media

www.LastBastionMedia.com

———————————

Publisher: Last Bastion Media, Texas, USA

Library of Congress Control Number: *Pending*

ISBN (Paperback/KDP Amazon): 978-1-970652-00-0

ISBN (Paperback/Wide Distribution via IngramSpark): 978-1-970652-04-8

ISBN (eBook/KDP Amazon): 978-1-970652-01-7

ISBN (eBook/Wide Distribution via Draft2Digital): 978-1-970652-05-5

ISBN (Hardcover/KDP Amazon): 978-1-970652-02-4

ISBN (Hardcover/Wide Distribution via IngramSpark): 978-1-970652-03-1

———————————

COPYRIGHT

First Edition, 2025

To Ricardo Rodriguez, Chief Motorcycle Instructor, BMW Performance Center, and my Brother in Christ, who taught me technical skills, helped me believe in my ability to enter the Adventure World, and has demonstrated God's grace and love since we first met.

To Tom Jenkins (deceased), CMA Ambassador, who introduced me to the Christian Motorcyclist Association, saved my life during my first bout of Guillain-Barre syndrome, and stayed with me through hours of medical delays despite great risk to his own health.

To Glenn Cunningham, my childhood neighbor and lifelong friend, who introduced me to the world of motorcycling, allowed me to have my first ride, and was an early inspiration for adventures of all types.

And to my wife, Sherry, who has given love and support throughout my adventure journey — and has rescued me from more than one critical situation of my own making.

CONTENTS

Preface		VII
1.	Love at First Sight	1
2.	Motocross Dreams	8
3.	All Things Are Possible	17
4.	Livin the SoCal Dream	28
5.	Thank God for Cold Weather	42
6.	The Rocket Bike	53
7.	Doing Without	61
8.	The Harley Years	68
9.	Back in the Game	92
10.	Adventure Bikes – The Plan	103
11.	International Motorcycle Show	111
12.	Las Vegas – Gear and All	119
13.	BMW Performance Center	129
14.	Backcountry Discovery	149

15. Adventure Training Camp   172

16. Lessons Learned   193

17. CMA and Beyond   201

Epilogue   222

Acknowledgements   223

About the author   224

Also by   226

PREFACE

This book began when I realized that I would have been far better off if I had known what I did not know during many of my adventures — and was lucky that I had learned what I had from my time in the Marine Corps, my time in the Royal Ambassadors (like a Baptist scouting organization), and my time studying motorcycle safety and survival in general.

The book is written based on my memories, and I make no claim that they are infallible. The reader may find recollections that don't seem to line up perfectly with prior reflections — and that's exactly how they are in my memory, not completely consistent.

Other than a typo that may have been missed, the spelling and capitalization inconsistencies that the reader may find are intentional. They reflect my ambivalence and lack of complete understanding regarding how to think about many things in the motorcycling world. (or is it in the Motorcycling World?)

The book finished as a reflection of many more things in my life than just motorcycling. If any part of the book can help even one person with anything in their life — whether motorcycling, adventure, or faith — the effort to complete it will have been well worth it.

Chapter One

LOVE AT FIRST SIGHT

Wow! I don't think I had ever seen anything like it before.

My next-door neighbor received a present that far surpassed anything that I had ever seen. And quite possibly, anything that I would ever get to own myself.

It had two wheels, an engine, and was painted a cool color, and looked like pure adventure. It was a mini-bike. Not a micro-motorcycle, like some of the other mini-bikes I would see and dream about in years to come, but a real 1960s style mini-bike.

It had what was essentially a lawn mower engine as its power plant, fat tires, a squatty frame, and it looked as though it could have been made in someone's garage, if they knew what they were doing.

You had to pull the rope-starter to crank the thing up, and when it started, it had a sweet sound and vibrating chain. The seat was a little vinyl-covered square of foam rubber, and I think it had a couple of small fenders.

This mini-bike was never going to make it onto any motocross tracks, and probably wouldn't even ever leave my friend's back-yard. But I would have given my left arm for it. And my right.

***

I think I was about 8 years old when the treasure arrived. My neighbor, Glenn, would have been about 11 or 12. We lived in a late 1960s middle-class neighborhood in a suburb of Atlanta, Georgia.

None of our houses had much room in them or in their yards, but we all did have back yards. And that was the track.

An oval around the pine trees is all that I can really remember. The grass got worn down, and it became a "single track oval." At the time, it looked plenty big enough to have fun on, but knowing how young minds exaggerate things, I'm sure it was tiny.

We all had chain link fences that separated our back yards, and I was reminded of that the first time I got the honor of riding the magnificent machine.

I don't know whether I begged and pleaded or just looked piti-ful, but my guess is that there was some combination of all of that.

I'm pretty sure that my parents didn't know anything about what I was being allowed to do, but then again, with all the times I had already been to the emergency room, and the times I would be in the future, maybe they did. Maybe they realized that the risk of serious injury in a tiny backyard was relatively small, I just don't remember.

Finally, the time came. I was allowed to sit on the bike while it was idling. I was reminded where the throttle was, but if I was told anything about the brakes or how to use them, I must have instantly forgotten what I was told.

I'm certain that I did not have a helmet, or eye protection, or gloves, or any type of protective equipment on, but who would have thought you would need it when all you're going to do is – hopefully – follow the oval around the trees.

They backed away, and I was alone with the metal-flaked steed. I gave it some gas, and I was off! Maybe a couple of miles per hour, but moving! And that's when things went wrong.

Apparently, I missed the part about turning or braking or not hitting the fence. As I recall, I drove straight ahead, headed for the chain link fence, and stopped because of the fence. No brakes were used in my demonstration of how a mini-bike could not break through a four-foot-tall, chain link fence.

Luckily, I was not injured. But unluckily, I was disallowed from continuing with this dream come true. I was done for the day. And probably the month, or two, or more.

I don't know for sure that I was ever allowed back on the amazing machine next door, but I think I was. Not much, but a little bit.

I'm pretty sure that I was, because I can remember one of my neighbor's friends – a little boy who was about the age of my neighbor – bringing his bike over to ride with my friend. I guess

they were going to have a sort of single-track, oval, very flat motocross track. One that was very small.

The friend had a Honda Trail 50, or at least that's what we called
them at the time. Now *this* was a micro-motorcycle — or at least
closer to it than what my neighbor had. And probably the first one
that I ever saw.

I don't remember the friend bringing it over more than once,
but he may have. I do remember that once again, the pitiful look,
etc. got me at least the chance to sit on it. In fact, I am pretty sure
that he let me drive it for maybe 20 feet.

I was in heaven.

From those first days forward, mini-bikes, micro-motorcycles,
and real motorcycles occupied a great deal of my thoughts.

***

I don't know whether I'm right or not, but I truly believe that there
are certain things that people have in their blood.

My wife has ridden horses from the time she was a small girl.
There are some very cute photos of her on her horses, when she
was about 5, wearing tiny red Keds, and a blond ponytail.

I don't mean she rode dude ranch horses a couple of times like I
did growing up, or in Summer Camp rode the nag around in the
circle, or went on a couple of $1.00 pony rides at the fair.

She rode horses, for real. She has countless stories of her and her
friends out riding through the country town and fields when they
were well below high school, and beyond.

She could not live without horses and horseback riding. It's in her blood.

I can take it or leave it.

My older brother began flying when he was about 14. I'm not sure when he got his official license, but he was young. I remember him taking me flying in a single-engine airplane when we couldn't have been more than 18 or 19 – and he was competent to take me up years before that.

My dad had stories of my brother wanting to go to the airport when he was very small, just to watch the airplanes take off and land. His interests always revolved around planes, and he flew from 14 on.

When he joined the Navy, he flew as a part of a flight crew on a P-3 Orion Sub-Chaser during the cold war. And he only did that, because he had been promised that he could finish college in the Navy and then become a Naval Aviator.

After the Navy, he went back to college and worked at an airport while he finished his degree. He eventually got into law enforcement and did quite a bit with aircraft there. Now, he is the Chief of Police at an International Airport.

He could not live without airplanes in his life. They are in his blood.

I have no interest in flying and never have.

For me, it's motorcycles. And it always has been.

The interesting part of it is that it's not just the riding. Yes, I like to ride motorcycles, but I would never be one of those guys who wins some award for the thousands and tens of thousands of miles he puts on his bike in a year.

Riding is just a part of it. And it always has been.

The way motorcycles look, the way they sound, the art forms that they are. All of it enthralls me. I love old classic bikes, bikes of the 60s and 70s, modern bikes, and futuristic bikes. I love street bikes, road racers, motocross bikes, Harleys, Indians, Japanese, European, and Adventure Bikes.

I love seeing and touching the real thing, and looking at photos. I love videos, films, and other art showing where bikes can take you – physically and mentally.

I could not live without bikes. I've tried. It's in my blood.

***

But in the late 1960s in that little Georgia suburban neighborhood, the ideas would just have to build. There was an older young man somewhere in our general area who had a jade green Suzuki.

Seeing him ride that beautiful bike through the tiny hills and around the gentle curves of our neighborhood was magical.

Easy Rider had come out sometime around then. Obviously, I was not going to be seeing it, and I don't even know if I knew it was out. But thinking back, that had to be the impetus for my mini-bike owning neighbor and another friend of his age to announce to all of us – and his parents – that after high school, their plans were to get motorcycles and strike out across the country.

They would just enjoy the scenery and make money from odd jobs along the way.

It sounded like a great idea, and I'm sure that I announced some plans to do likewise when and if I got old enough.

The last memory I have from those very early days is of one of my elementary school teachers inviting the class over to her house for an end-of-the-year party, and her husband having a motorcycle.

I don't remember much about it, and I'm not even sure that I have that part right. But I do remember that the bike was black, and looking back, it was a classic street bike of that day.

I don't know whether everyone in the class was given a ride, but my memory is that I was. It was a short ride, and probably lasted no longer than a minute or two, but it was great.

I needed more.

CHAPTER TWO

MOTOCROSS DREAMS

We moved back to Florida in 1971. I was 10.

I had never gotten a mini-bike while in Georgia, but still loved them – them being anything on two wheels. I still dreamed of one day having a mini-bike or motorcycle of my own.

While in Georgia, I had a pretty bad crash on a bicycle, so even if my parents had ever thought about me having a mini-bike as a possibility prior to that time, I'm sure they weren't thinking that afterward.

When I say pretty bad, I mean knocked unconscious for about 30 minutes, teeth knocked out, and various other things that happen when you jump off a moving vehicle and land on your face, on concrete.

I was blessed that I had not been hurt any worse, given the totality of the circumstances, and while Mom and Dad may have been worried for my safety, I certainly wasn't. I wanted a mini-bike. Desperately.

In 6th grade, I switched schools, and began riding a bus. What that did was expose me to a whole new crop of kids, many of whom loved motorcycles too. And more than that, many had parents who indulged their desires.

Riding the bus and having all that time to talk with other kids about bikes, I learned – or thought I learned – a great deal. I knew all about the Japanese bikes that were all the craze and, at that point, still fairly new in the U.S.

"Kawasakis are a piece of junk. They're inexpensive, but no good.[1]"

"Hondas are okay, but they are boring.[2]"

"Yamahas and Suzukis are awesome! They look cool and don't fall apart."

"What are these others – Bultaco? Combat Wombat?? Husqvarna???"

Then, about 7th or 8th grade, one of the older kids started riding his motorcycle to school. All of us on the bus would see him zoom by, and wish that was us. He looked cool and he had a blue, Suzuki 125 – an on-off bike. That's what we called them.

---

1. I have since owned at least three and have loved them. Turns out they are **not** junk!

2. I have since owned at least five and have loved every one of them. Turns out they are not boring, but rather very reliable.

Wow! That is so cool! I want to have a motorcycle to ride to school too, when I get old enough!

Of course, he had done it one better – he wasn't old enough. He was 14.

In those days, in Florida, you could get a "Learner's Permit" at 15 years of age. Once you had that, with no further testing, you were authorized to ride a motorcycle on the road, as long as it was "under 5 brake horsepower."

"What's a 'brake' horsepower?"

"I don't know, but all the 125 models are under it."

So, we all knew that we could ride a 125 on the street, if it was a street-legal bike, once we were 15 and got our Learner's Permit.

His bike was legal for the street. He wasn't.

As the story goes, his parents bought him the Suzuki to ride around in the fields close to our houses. Maybe the plan was that once he was 15, he would ride it to school.

He figured, "Why wait?"

And he looked cool, with his long hair and smile, zooming by on that bike every day. Until the police caught him, and that was the end of that. He was done, at least for quite a while.

Nevertheless, he was part of the motorcycle-this and motorcycle-that all around me those days.

My friends and I would buy magazines and look at all the cool photos of the bikes and riders. I had motorcycle toys, and I could watch all the older kids around the neighborhood get their bikes – and learn more about all the models from watching them.

There were incredible, unbelievable stories about various neighborhood legends, and the things they could do on their bikes. And tales of the big superstars that were emerging in the real race world.

Motocross was where it was at. Motocross riders were the coolest, and the toughest, and the most like superheroes. This was not the jammed-together Supercross or Arenacross that developed later, this was real motocross.

Super fast straightaways, huge jumps, whoop-de-dos, and giant berms. The tracks played out over a large area – way too much to put into a single stadium or anything that size.

It was dangerous, it was fast, and it was something that I wanted to learn to do.

As I got into my early teens, I had a friend that had a legit BMX bike. And this was in the days way before most people had even seen one.

His bike was a yellow "mono-shock," and it was built specifically for BMX. It had the proper handlebars, the grip pedals, the solo seat, etc. And he knew how to ride it.

He could jump down small flights of stairs on the bike, bunny hop over curbs, ride wheelies, and do all the stuff that I wished I could do.

Fortunately, I had a bicycle that could be converted to a BMXish-type bike. Somehow, I came up with the money to buy a proper seat – probably used – and pedals. Then, as luck would have it, I found a pair of BMX handlebars lying in a field while out riding one day. Presto, I had a BMX bike too!

The only problem was that I was about as athletic as a bowling ball is buoyant. I never could ride wheelies more than a couple of feet, couldn't figure out how to bunny hop, and could not jump down things or off of things with my bike – not to amount to anything.

But none of that stopped my dreams.

We would ride our BMX bikes literally all over town. And often to the motorcycle dealerships.

Many a Saturday afternoon would find us having ridden several miles over to Hap's Honda to stare at and dream about the motocross bikes and on-off bikes that they had in inventory.

More than that, we could get some of their brochures that had pictures and sales pitches for all of their bikes.

By then, Honda had gone past the Trail 50 and Trail 70. While I would still gladly have taken one of those, if that was all I could get, they now had little miniature 50cc and 70 or 75cc motocross bikes! They looked just like the big bikes, at least to me.

I have no idea how much they cost back then, but I know that I knew at the time. And I knew they were far out of my reach.

My family was not wealthy. In fact, quite the opposite.

While there were certainly plenty of people poorer than us, we didn't have extra money to spend on expensive "toys" and my parents made sure that I knew it.

I vividly recall the feeling of looking at and dreaming about the possibility of getting a Honda XR 50. I just stared at the brochure and tried to picture myself having one and all the fun I would have with it.

I'm pretty sure that by that age — 13 or so — I would not have fit very well on a 50 and would have needed the XR 75, but since the 50 was out of the realm of possibility cost-wise, the 75 wasn't even worth fantasizing about.

My dad was out of town for a month, working on his doctorate degree, and for some reason, I rationalized that when he returned, maybe he would want to by me an XR 50. Maybe if I talked to him about it enough, he would decide that getting me an expensive toy was a great idea. I just needed to pray and hope enough.

Dad returned, the subject was broached, and the hope was gone in a nanosecond. There was no way and no how. Even if I somehow figured out a way to make money myself, there was no way that I was going to be allowed to own a motorcycle.

The fact that by that time, I thought that maybe my life's ambition would be to become a professional motocross rider didn't matter. They were too dangerous and too expensive. I could not have one now; I could not have one ever.

I'm sure that news brought a great many tears, and I can remember being crestfallen. But I had been poor my whole life. Even by that age, there had been plenty of things that I wanted and not been able to have. This was just one more thing.

Motocross was still in my future. I just had to believe.

***

Maybe the route to go was like so many other kids around me were going — an Enduro, a Trail bike, an on-off. Any one of those would allow me to be the Motocross rider of my dreams once I got to the dirt, and allow me to get myself there without needing anyone or anything else to help me.

Mom at least met me halfway. Well, maybe not halfway. Maybe 2% or 3% of the way. She bought me one or two subscriptions to motorcycle magazines. I could get those every month, pore over the articles, look at all the photos and ads and continue to dream. Additionally, I could learn.

The articles that I read most carefully were the ones about how to stay alive on a motorcycle. They talked about where to position yourself on the road, what to look out for, and what type of gear to wear.

It wasn't that I was concerned about getting hurt – I wasn't. But that was not because I was such a good rider (or going to be such a good rider) that I would be better than getting hurt. It was because I had an unshakable knowledge that my life was in God's hands. Nothing was going to happen to me that wasn't part of the plan – and that included all of the trips to the Emergency Room that I took.

We were very fortunate in those days. There was still open space around Florida, and the Police still had a sense of humor.

What that meant was that there were several large fields near where all us kids lived, and the police didn't bother us, as long as we stayed off the roads.

I was also fortunate in that I had a number of friends who were far luckier than I was when it came to having parents with a more cavalier attitude about their health. True, my parents weren't going to buy me a motorcycle, or even allow me to buy one, but if I could get the other kids to let me ride theirs, it would at least make life bearable.

Some kids did and some kids didn't. And so life went.

Yamaha made some kind of 80cc Enduro at that time, and one of my friends from church had a dad who got him one. As the story goes, he didn't even really want one that badly, but he threatened or talked about quitting baseball — which his dad loved — and his dad bought it as a way to bribe him into continuing to play.

I think he let me ride it alone a couple of times, but my biggest memory is riding on the back as he drove it around. That wasn't great, but it was something.

An older couple at church that had older kids who were now out of the house had a mini-bike that they had bought their kids and it was now in storage at their house just going to waste. They invited me over one day after church to ride it around. Once.

The next door neighbor kid had a dad with custody of him after a divorce, back when that kind of thing never happened. That kid didn't even like motorcycles or talk about them that much — his dad bought him a 100cc Honda Enduro. He hadn't even asked for one.

And on and on it went.

This kid had one because he was rich. That kid had one because of his parents' marital status. Another kid had one for who knows what reason. But I didn't and wasn't going to.

In retrospect, maybe it made some sense.

I have a vivid memory of one kid in the neighborhood whose dad — the subject of some interesting rumors — bought him a legit street bike to ride "with all the kids" up in the pine-needle-covered field near all our houses.

Anyone that has ridden on pine needles knows that they are not the place for street tires, but regardless, that's what he had. And for some reason he let me ride it one day.

I saw my dad sitting in his car — probably coming home from work — pulled over to see what all these kids were doing in this field, and no doubt looking for me. As a parent now, I'm sure he was checking to make sure that I wasn't a part of anything stupid.

At that exact moment, I had a brilliant idea. With no helmet on, riding a street bike with street tires on slippery pine needles, I would zoom across the field as fast as I could go, in order to say hi to Dad. So, I took off.

I remember looking down and seeing the speedometer hitting at least 50 mph, before I slowed to pull up to Dad.

My father did not cuss. He was a Baptist Minister and never said a bad word. And he didn't then. But he was literally shaking when I pulled up, and he told me in no uncertain terms to get off that motorcycle immediately and go home. Which is exactly what I did.

But I still wanted to be a Motocross Racer.

CHAPTER THREE

ALL THINGS ARE POSSIBLE

Then it happened!

I have no idea why, but it happened!!

I had long ago stopped asking Mom and Dad to buy me a motorcycle. I was now 16 and working a legit job at the grocery store.

I didn't need them to buy me one. I just needed them to allow me to buy one for myself. I could earn the money and would, if only given a chance.

Given how it changed my life, I can't believe that I can't remember the exact conversation, but I can't. I just know that it happened. Somehow, some way, all of the begging and pleading and promising and tears and sincerity had worked. Mom and Dad changed their minds. I could buy a motorcycle.

More than that, I could buy one that I could ride to school. I could get the coveted on-off bike, like so many of my friends had

had — even before they could legally ride them on the street — and have all my dreams come true. I could ride to school and I could ride to fields, and I could start learning to be a motocross rider. A real dirt rider.

Now, what could I afford?

I don't remember how much money I had, but somehow I had saved some from my job sacking groceries. I was paid minimum wage, and at that time, it was somewhere just north of $2.00 per hour, so I know I didn't have much.

My dad took me to the dealership to look at bikes, and I don't even remember which dealership, but I was looking strictly at used bikes. I'm pretty sure that's because I had calculated that that was all I could afford. This would have been the time that some good parental guidance could have come in handy, but my dad knew nothing of motorcycles.

I'm not sure if he also didn't know anything about used vehicle salesmen who take advantage of idiots, but if he did, he didn't share it with me. This salesman must have seen me coming from a mile away.

I left the dealership that day with a piece of junk that any honest person would have been embarrassed to foist on some kid, but not that guy. I'm sure that he and his buddies had a good laugh about the stooge who bought that Orange Pile of Trouble.

By make, it was a Suzuki. And I know for a fact that Suzuki makes some outstanding machines these days, and may have even back then. But I didn't care shortly after this purchase, and I don't care now. That bike soured me on Suzukis from then until now, and that purchase was over 45 years ago.

This Orange Monster was orange because the original gas tank had been replaced by some huge, plastic, orange tank, which I'm sure would have been good to have on the proper bike. In addition to that, it had knobby tires, and the look of a dirt bike that may be able to pass the inspection needed to ride it on the road — if I bought and attached a bicycle horn to it. And I'm not kidding.

Why my dad allowed me to waste my money on that bike I'll never know, but I did, and it was pretty much a pain in the neck from the outset.

The carburetor didn't function properly, and that's coming from someone who knows next to nothing about carburetors. It rarely ran well, but it was all mine, and I was far better off than I had ever been.

I know that I rode it to school at least a couple of times, because I remember one time having to ride with the knobby tires, both during and after some rain.

Luckily, having read those motorcycle magazines for years, and particularly the parts about how to stay alive, I made sure to always have my helmet and gloves, and was smart enough to realize the caution I needed on a wet road with knobbies.

Nevertheless, the Orange Beast was not a keeper. It didn't take long for me to realize that I wanted something more reliable, something better looking, and something that I could love and be proud of.

Now that the seal had been broken, all I had to do was explain to mom and dad that I wanted to trade in the Orange Junk Pile and get something better, which I did.

***

I can remember it like it was yesterday. I'm not sure why I had decided that Yamahas were the best bikes made — or at least the best that I could afford — but I had. Yamaha had the DT series, and it was exactly what I wanted.

At that point in my life, I still had a fear of bigger bikes, or at least bigger cc bikes. I'm not sure where the fear came from, since the reality was that the difference between a DT 125 and a DT 175 and a DT 250, etc., was probably negligible for my anticipated usage, but I had it. So, I decided that a DT 175 was the bike for me.

That year — 1978, I think — the 175 came in Red with Black accent or Blue with Silver accent. The dealership had one of each on the showroom floor. I am not sure if I had decided prior to getting to the dealership, but once there, I decided on the Red one. I nervously asked if I could take it for a test ride, and the salesman said yes.

If I were in Sarasota now, I could probably take you to almost the exact spot where I first hit the pavement, when I found out how slippery sand on asphalt is.

I had ridden the brand new, beautiful Red bike no more than a few hundred yards from the dealership, and was still on some form of parking lot of a neighboring business, when I went to make a left U-turn. As I did, I gave the bike gas, right as I had my back tire over some sand, and in the blink of an eye, I was on my back, and my helmeted head hit the pavement.

I picked the bike up, dusted myself off, rode the bike back to the dealership, handed the key to the salesman and announced that I would love to make the purchase — of the Blue one.

My dad, inexplicably, tried to talk me into getting a purely street bike like the 250 model that he saw on the showroom floor, and to this day, I'm baffled. In my mind, there was almost no way to get killed in the dirt, and a myriad of ways on the street.

I know that he was smart enough to know this to some extent, because he had made me swear to a whole set of rules about where and how I would ride. And looking back, all of those were very good rules — they may well have kept me alive for so long as they were in effect.

Why there was no rule about not speeding, I'm not sure, but I guess maybe he just assumed that I would have the good sense to go an appropriate speed. Looking back, I didn't.

I remember every morning getting to finally be that cool kid that I used to see out the bus window riding to school. Since Dad made me promise to stay on back roads, I had the perfect excuse to ride right by all of the bus stops, but I'm pretty sure I would have anyway. How else would all the younger kids see how cool I was?[1]

---

1. For the record: They couldn't, because I wasn't.

I had a blue and silver, brand new Yamaha DT 175 and a yellow Bell Moto Star full-face helmet, and I zoomed by every morning going at least 50 in the 30 or 35 zone.

Better than all that, I had the ability to ride my bike to the fields and pretend I was a motocross star, and actually try to learn the things I would have to know to become one.

***

I would start every day by jumping my bike off the small jump onto the street in front of our house, and zoom to school. I was now one of the owners of a bike and not just a watcher and wisher any longer.

At various times, groups of us would gather up at the biggest field around, with its pine trees surrounding the edges and inhabiting some of the interiors.

We didn't have any particular plan, and there was no track. But there were a few small jumps. Very small jumps. Jumps that were perfect for someone like me who had almost killed himself on a jump with his BMX bike a couple years earlier.

One day, when I was still about 14, the friend with the Mono Shock and I decided that we should build a sweet jump right in front of my house — in the street.

Although I took a great many math classes in high school and at least one physics class, apparently I didn't understand trajectories, angles, and gravity. And I didn't have many, if any, riding skills.

My Mono Shock friend zoomed toward the jump, which had been built with a ramp that was far too short and steep, and went up, flew through the air looking cool, and landed perfectly.

Now it was my turn.

I am as certain as I can be that it was God looking out for me when I had the sudden thought that maybe I should go inside and grab the football helmet that I had owned since I was seven.

It barely fit, and I never wore it on my bike before of after this ride, but I praise God that I wore it that day.

I zoomed toward the steep ramp as fast as I could go, without a care in the world, certain that I would look as cool as my friend just had.

Instead, I went straight up the ramp, made a U-turn in mid-air, and went straight down onto my front tire and over the handlebars, at a steep angle, driving my head straight into the asphalt street.

I am certain that the only thing that kept me out of the Emergency Room, if not worse, was the Sears, black and yellow, 1968 style football helmet.

**

Now it was two or so years later. I had a real motorcycle, and could ride it in the fields with my friends, as we worked on our dirt skills.

And you would think that the lesson about the helmet saving my life would have made a firm impression. You'd be wrong.

For some reason, I firmly believed that helmets were needed when riding a motorcycle on the street, in part because they were legally required. But more than that, I had read and understood that a crash on the street, even at relatively slow speeds, without a helmet, could be deadly. Stupidly, I believed that helmets when riding off-road were optional.

I know that, and remember it vividly, because of another of my many trips to the ER.

One day, as a bunch of us were riding up in the big field, one of the rich kids brought his Honda 3-Wheeled ATV up to the field.

These days, a person has to be fairly old to even remember those things. They were taken off the market after not too many years, having caused quite a few injuries — many of them serious.

There was kind of a "trick" to riding them, and I didn't know the trick. But I wanted to try it, and now — as a motorcycle owner — I had something to trade.

For years, I had just had to beg or look pitiful in order to get a friend to allow me a couple minutes on his bike, but now I no longer did.

The rich kid and I made a trade — "You can ride my motorcycle for awhile, while I ride the ATV."

For the life of me, I cannot figure out what I did with my helmet. Maybe I stupidly let the rich kid borrow it, along with the bike, thinking that the ATV was so safe that there was no way I would need one.

Shortly after the trade, I drove the ATV, full speed, right into a pine tree that was about three feet in diameter. When I did, I was helmetless and it was only the Grace of God that saved me from another serious head injury. Instead, I drove my shoulder into the tree and was certain that I had broken it. Fortunately, X-rays showed that I had not.

***

I rode that DT the rest of my junior year and over the summer. I'm pretty sure that it helped me get one of my first girlfriends, because I would come zooming up to Vacation Bible School and slide to a stop and park it in a safe spot — that just happened to be where all the kids could see it, and of course know how cool I was for owning it.

Somewhere along the line, I realized that driving a car can be more practical than taking the bike everywhere, so the DT quit being a daily commute vehicle to school and whichever job I was holding at the time.

I know that I didn't ride it to school daily my senior year, because I remember driving my dad's VW, but I still loved the Blue and Silver Beauty.

I would wash it and wax it and change the oil regularly and lube and adjust the chain, probably more often than it needed. I babied it and loved it. And then graduation came and it was time for college.

The DT went with me to Baylor University, in Waco, Texas, being pulled behind our small car on some kind of contraption that had the front wheel suspended, but the back tire on the ground.

I recall having to remove the chain, but I knew how to do things like that back then.[2]

The bike did not get as much use my freshman year, because I lived on campus in a dormitory. Worse though, it had to live outside for the first time in its life. So, it was subjected to all the rain and harsh weather that hit us that year, which broke my heart, since I loved that bike.

Looking back, I guess to some extent that was my first experience being an Adventure Rider — in the sense that I would often go on adventures on my bike. At least they were adventures to me.

Living on campus, having never been to Waco prior to my first day of Orientation, and not looking at a map, I really had no idea about the world around me. So on weekends, often on Sundays, I would take off on my bike alone, to go explore. I don't know where all I went, but I remember riding for a couple of hours or so, and enjoying the feeling of getting myself "lost."

I wasn't lost in the "I'm in the middle of Utah and I missed a turn and went down some road that my GPS doesn't even recognize as a road" sense. I was just lost in the sense that I had no idea where I was, but knew that I was somewhere in Waco.

And knowing that meant that I also knew that Waco had exactly one tall building — tall enough that with Waco's flat topography, the building could be seen from a long way off. I recall the enjoy-

---

2. In more recent years, I have tried my best to never touch tools of any kind. We don't get along.

able feeling of riding and stopping and standing as tall as I could on my foot pegs and looking all around to see if I could see the Alico Building. When I would finally see it, a long way off, I would head in that direction until I found my way back to familiar streets and make my way home. It was fun, and felt adventurous, at least to a degree.

At the end of my freshman year, I knew that I was headed for Marine Corps Officer training that summer, and I had to make a decision about my beloved DT 175. It was still beautiful and ran like a top, and I still loved it, but life was busy and getting busier. Besides that, I always needed money. So I sold it. Sadly, I took a few hundred dollars cash from an older student, and let him take the first of many bikes that I wish I still had today.

The real devastation came at the beginning of the next school year when I saw my bike somewhere in town. The guy who bought it did not love it, as I had, and he had trashed it. I couldn't believe it.

I love bikes far too much to ever abuse any bike like the new guy had abused my first love. The bike that I had kept in near-showroom condition and babied for years was now reduced to an eyesore, and it obviously bothers me to this day.

CHAPTER FOUR

LIVIN THE SOCAL DREAM

A great deal happened between the time I sold my DT and the end of college.

In the same summer that I sold my baby, I bought my first car. It was not a brand-new, from-the-showroom, beauty. It was a small, used Honda Civic, with no air conditioning. Nevertheless, what it meant was that I had a vehicle, and I certainly did not have the finances, or probably time, to get another bike.

I made it through my Sophomore year probably without ever getting on a bike, and didn't have withdrawal symptoms to any degree. By my Junior year, though, I had some need for a bike, and luckily had a friend who had a classic street bike — a Yamaha 600 or 650.

The friend was a fraternity brother, and let me borrow the bike on a fairly regular basis, just for fun. Being a bigger bike, it allowed me to take girls on riding dates, which were great because that allowed me to both have a cheap date, and ride.

Unfortunately, at some point, the friend's bike was stolen, and that put an end to my riding again. I think that the theft was towards the beginning of my Senior year, and by that time, I was either engaged or about to be, and had a lot of other things on my mind.

I finished that year, graduated, and got commissioned as a Second Lieutenant in the United States Marine Corps.

From Waco, my fiancé and I headed to El Paso, then — as newly-weds — to Quantico, Virginia. The first year in the Marine Corps was in Northern Virginia and Lawton, Oklahoma, for Artillery training. I was too busy and poor in Virginia to own a bike, and still too poor in Oklahoma.

Our vehicles were a horrendously ugly Toyota Station Wagon that we had "inherited," and a brand new, over-priced, Dodge Colt — the cheapest car we could find. Both of those cars went with us to Oklahoma, and then with us to Southern California, when I got stationed at Camp Pendleton, in Northern San Diego County.

The weather in California was beautiful, and I don't mean only on some days. It was beautiful, it seemed, about 99% of the time. So, it was awesome riding weather. But, at least initially, we still had the poverty issue.

One day, as I had the Toyota parked in front of my office at Camp Las Pulgas, where Artillery lived at that time at Camp Pendleton, my Commanding Officer and I walked by it, on the way to a meeting.

As we walked, the CO stated for whomever else was walking with us, and for my benefit too, "I think my Legal Officer needs to drive a little bit bigger piece of _____ than this," and pointed at my car — and he didn't use the word "junk."

Luckily, by that time, I had been in the Corps long enough that I had a few extra dollars every month, that I hadn't had previously. Given that what I did for a living was already a pretty dangerous thing, and that I was young and figured I'd live forever, the decision was made that the "piece of" junk should be gotten rid of and I should get a motorcycle to ride as transportation.

By then, I had been without a bike for about five years, and hadn't been keeping up with the models that were available.

Although I had once seen a rider in Florida on an on-off bike with tags from somewhere up North, I know that I felt like what I needed was a bigger, street bike. I had to have something to keep up easily with traffic on the Southern California freeways that I would be using for my commute.

***

I recall going to the Yamaha dealership and trying to decide between the Virago 700 and the Maxim 700. I don't remember knowing what the difference was between the two at that time, and I'm pretty sure that I picked the Virago because of the styling. The cruiser style looked good to me, and I recall it being a very comfortable bike to ride.

The real question, though, is why I did not pick the Virago 1100, which would have made infinitely more sense on the freeways, where most of my riding would be done. I know it had nothing to do with weight concerns, since in those days, I didn't even think of those things. But it may have had to do with money. Certainly the price difference could not have been much, but those were the days when my wife and I were making decisions based upon less than $10.00 per month difference.

Another reason for the choice, though, I'm sure was my remaining trepidation about larger cc bikes and whether I could "handle" them. As at the time of the DT purchase years earlier, I know that I had serious misgivings about my ability to confidently ride a bike that I perceived as being as powerful as I thought the 1100 must be. Looking back, and knowing what I know now, it made no sense, but the thoughts were there.

***

The Virago was an awesome bike, and I loved it. Like the DT, it ran like a top and was extremely reliable and fun to ride.

Being that the bike was a "cruiser," it certainly did not add to any off-road aspect of my adventure journey, but it did give me extremely valuable riding experience in terms of miles under my belt, and it did allow me to have a few adventurous rides.

I know that I put about 35 miles per day on the bike, and that would be divided about half and half between freeway and the winding road leading from the freeway to my office. I did that

pretty much every weekday for about 2 years — when I wasn't
in the field — so I guess when you do the math, that could have
come out to over 18,000 miles. I'm not sure that it did, when
you deduct the days that I was in the field, but even if I was just
close to that, it means that I put more miles on that Virago by
the time I left California than I have put on any other bike I
have ever owned, and more in that amount of time than at any
other point in my life.

I recall riding on one magical adventure one weekend, up
into the mountains, somewhere not too far from where we
lived. I have no idea where it was, and I'm certain that the
"mountains" were hills, but Southern California does have
some really cool areas to explore. With my wife on the back, we
set off one Saturday afternoon, and rode at what was probably
not the safest time — at dusk and after.

We ended up finding one of those out-of-the-way eating es-
tablishments in which memories are made. There was nothing
about the entire situation that made it memorable, other than
the fact that I was on the bike, on winding roads, and found
somewhere that I had not set out for. Somewhere perfect.

It had the same feel that I had in Waco, except that I had
someone to share it with, and I certainly was not trying to get
lost. It felt great.

***

At one point, several of the other Officers in the Artillery Battalion got cruisers such that there were now about six or seven of us who could ride together. For at least one other Lieutenant, motorcycles had been a part of his life. He knew what he was doing. For the others, it was apparently a newer experience, but something they wanted to try.

Like with the ride in the mountains, I have a pretty vivid memory of all of us taking off on a couple of occasions at lunch time, to ride through the winding roads and hills of Camp Pendleton. Since we were all Artillery, we worked in the 43 Area, which was somewhat centrally located on the massive base.

Pendleton was so large and there were so many different Camps within it, for all the various parts of the First Marine Division, that there was more than one Officers' Club. I don't recall how many there were, but I know that there would have been at least one at main side, but it wouldn't have been much fun to ride to. That would be like choosing to go for a group ride, directly into slow-moving traffic.

The most awesome club that we knew of was at one of the Northernmost camps. I don't remember which Camp it was, but I know that it had one of the cool names that all of them did, like San Mateo or Camp Onofre. And of course the name didn't matter. What mattered was the camaraderie of riding for the first time with a large group on an adventure.

With no cell phones and no GPS, we would take off on the route that the leader wanted to take us on.

Although I have many fond memories of my time in the Marine Corps, there was not a great deal of time that was spent on fun. This was fun!

I can still see the line of bikes winding along the road, through the curves, and making it to the kind of place that you would fantasize about being able to hang out with your fellow brothers-in-arms. The Club was a smaller operation than a Mainside O-Club would be. It was something akin to a modern sports bar, but without the need to entice civilians to come in and eat. This place was just for Marines and any others that had permission to be on the base, such as Navy Doctors.

The food wasn't memorable, and neither was the conversation. But what was memorable to this day is the feeling of setting out to a quasi-unknown location on an iron horse with my brothers.

***

The most memorable adventure that I had with my Virago while on active duty was taking it to the Marine Corps Air Ground Combat Center at 29 Palms, California.

Though I had gotten the job as the Legal Officer of the Artillery Battalion, my primary Military Occupational Specialty was still Artillery. I would work on Legal matters most days, but at certain times, I still went to the Field or other training in support of various other combat units, such as 1st Battalion, 7th Marines.

For some reason, the particular training that led to my big adventure only required one Officer from the Artillery unit to attend, and so I was all alone, going to join up with the other Command Staff from 1st Tanks or 1st LAVs, I don't remember which.

What that meant was that I did not have to travel with a unit. As a Lieutenant, I was responsible for getting myself from Camp Pendleton to 29 Palms. That gave me the perfect opportunity to take my bike on a long-distance ride! (Or at least what seemed a long distance to me.)

When convoys would travel from Camp Las Pulgas to 29 Palms, it could take six hours or more. Early in my time at Pendleton, due to the time spent in convoys, I thought that the trip from Pulgas to the Palms must be hundreds of miles.

What I eventually figured out was that it was a trip of only about 180 miles. It took forever due to the gearing of the jeeps, and the fact that we drove at speeds that must have been under 30 miles per hour.

***

So the plan was to take my first long ride on a bike ever. A ride that would require me to plan and pack and think about things that I had never had to think about on a bike before.

I don't remember a lot about the actual ride out to the Palms and back, except for one very significant thing, and it would add to my knowledge base that comes in handy to this day. Wind can be miserable and even dangerous.

Having driven cross-county on more than one occasion by the time of my 29 Palms trip, I had surely encountered strong winds at various times. But I had always been in a car.

Yes, wind can affect driving in a car, but in that enclosed bubble, one is always relatively safe. At least compared to being out there on a bike.

I don't know exactly where I was, but it was on some road akin to a freeway, if not an actual freeway. It was out in the middle of nowhere, and thankfully, there were not many vehicles on the road. And it was getting dark.

This was on the trip out, and I had miscalculated my riding time, so I was still riding when I should have already been there, from a safety standpoint.

I vividly recall riding and trying to maintain proper freeway speeds, all while literally being blown over. I had never before ridden a bike in an environment wherein I had to try to maintain a straight path, while leaning into the wind at what felt like a 45-degree angle.

Going faster didn't seem to help, and slowing down felt like I could be blown over completely. The idea of stopping seemed pointless at best and dangerous at worst. So, I kept going, and praying that I would get to my destination or the wind would stop.

I finally made it, and was done with the wind, at least for then. To this day, I would rather ride in a pouring rain storm than in wind as strong as I had in Southern California that night.

I don't have any idea how strong the wind actually was, but it vacillated between very discomforting and scary. When I listen to riders talk about the winds that can be encountered on some of the roads heading down to Ushuaia in Argentina, I empathize and never listen dismissively. I never want to ride in that kind of wind again.[1]

***

Overall, my years riding in Southern California were great. The weather, the scenery, most everything was awesome. But not everything.

These were the Top Gun years. I was living in Southern California when the first Top Gun movie was filmed. More importantly, it was being filmed right where I was, and when it was released, the whole riding world could be envious of the riding environment that I had out my front door.

Many of the scenes were filmed in the City of San Diego, which was a few miles away, but we frequented it and were familiar with all the spots. But at least some of the motorcycle footage of Tom Cruise was filmed in Northern San Diego County, in Oceanside, right where I rode.

In the scene where he zooms away from Kelly McGillis' house and has the beach and palm trees buzzing by on his left, he was

---

1. Last Chapter spoiler alert: You don't always get what you want.

in Oceanside. In fact, if he had kept going for about another half mile, when the scene cut off, he would have been at my door.

Those were good years to be in the Military — the mid-1980s — and being in the Marines was the best. Being young, in awesome shape, and having a perfect bike to cruise around the beaches and hills of Southern California could make for some amazing memories. But in typical Marine Corps fashion, the service made sure that it wasn't too good. To some extent, they even made it a little miserable.

The years I was on active duty were not the Sgt. Rock years. This was not the WWII, Korea, or even the Vietnam Marine Corps. This was the Peacetime Corps. And the Peacetime Corps loved making rules.

If you are a Commanding Officer, and there is no fighting to command, you can command by coming up with more and more rules. And rules in the military have the weight of law. A violation of the rules is a violation of the law, and could end one up in serious trouble.

The Marine Corps did not want any Marine to get injured. That seems really silly, given what we did for a living, but that's the way it was. Getting injured on liberty just means that you are not available when you're supposed to be on duty. Getting killed on liberty is really upsetting to COs. It could make them look bad, which could affect their Fitness Reports, which could affect their career, which they did not like.

So, what that meant was that the Marine Corps was very against motorcycles. They couldn't or wouldn't outright ban them, but they could and would make you think twice or more about getting one.

"Hi, Marine Corps, I just bought myself a motorcycle, and I need to ride it to my house on base."

"You can't ride on base until you take a Motorcycle Safety Course."

"Okay, where do I take the Course?"

"It's offered on base, every month."

"How do I get to the course on base, if I can't ride to the course on base, until I have taken the course on base? And oh yeah, what am I supposed to do with my motorcycle between now and the time the course starts, since I live on base, and I can't bring my bike on base to my house?"

What a pain. But, again, that was typical.

I don't remember all the details, but somehow there was a way to get a special permission slip issued by someone to allow you to ride your bike through the base gate and to your house, where you were not allowed to ride from until it was time to start the Safety Course.

When the date for the Safety Course came, you could use your permission slip to ride from your house to the Course and back, for however many days the course lasted — but no other riding was allowed!!! Heaven forbid you practice your riding skills.

Once the course was over, you could take your graduation certificate to somewhere on base and get the sticker that would allow you to ride on base just as though you were in your automobile.

But that wasn't the end of it.

You could certainly argue that from a safety standpoint, the other Marine Corps rule made sense. As I've gotten older, I have bought into the ATGATT way of riding — All The Gear, All The Time.

Accidents are going to happen, and if they do when you are wearing flip flops, or a t-shirt with no jacket, or no gloves, or shorts, or no helmet, you can end up really really sorry. Everyone knows that. And in my opinion, only a simpleton would ever ride a bike without eye protection at anytime.

But, all that being said, there are times when riding in a non-ATGATT way is not much, if any, more dangerous than riding a bicycle would be. For example, there was a gym in our neighborhood that could easily be ridden to at a very slow speed, and in a manner not substantially different than being on a bicycle. To have to do what the Marine Corps required at all times — wear long pants, leather boots, a jacket, gloves, and a helmet to go to a quick workout or just down the street to the beach, seemed a little overkill. Regardless, those were the rules.

Oh, and there was one more rule. Was this final rule just meant to make us riders so irritated and embarrassed by it that we wouldn't ride — or wouldn't ride as much? I'll never know.

What did I like about my neighbor's mini bike? It was cool.

What did I like about Motocross racers? They were cool.

What did I love about my DT 175 and zooming around on it? It felt cool.

What would riding a Virago all around Southern California be when you are in your twenties, have life by the tail, and are a Marine Corps Officer when that was admired by society?

Well, you would think it would be really cool. The Marine Corps wasn't about to allow that.

"At all times, day and night, on base and off, when riding any motorcycle, in addition to all other mandated safety gear, all riders MUST wear an Orange and Yellow highly reflective vest."

"Here, think you're going to go out and cruise around and look cool? Think again. Wear this: look like a nerd."

CHAPTER FIVE

THANK GOD FOR COLD WEATHER

I drove out of Southern California in the fall of 1987 while listening to California Dreamin' by the Mamas and the Papas, and behind the wheel of the largest Hertz Penske rental truck available. The truck was packed with far more stuff than it was supposed to hold, and one of those things was my precious Virago.

I had made it through all the miles and all the traffic of California, and was now headed for much calmer things in Waco, Texas — again.

I was back. Back at Baylor, back in school, and back with a motorcycle being my primary form of transportation, as a student.

The difference this time was that I was not in a dorm. I was married, four years out of undergrad, and starting law school. My wife and I lived in a rental house across town from the school, and I would be riding my bike virtually daily.

And though we left Camp Pendleton in the fall of 1987, the trip back to Waco was a long and circuitous one.

Originally, the plan was that I would attend the University of Florida law school, and my riding days would be in Gainesville, Florida. We moved all of the things in the back of the Hertz to Gainesville, except my bike, and went on a sort of vacation to await school to begin in January.

During that time, I rode my bike some in and around Sarasota, and in looking back, I have always regretted not using that time for more adventure. I don't know if it was because I was anxious about school starting relatively soon, or just the dimwittedness of youth and thinking that there was always "tomorrow" to take this trip or that.

I know my wife and I rode a couple places locally, but those days would have been a fantastic time to ride all the way around Florida, and visit all the places in the State that I still would like to see. We didn't.

Stupidly, we wasted a lot of time, and I worked a little to earn a few dollars.

During that time, I did ride my bike for transportation to the worst job I ever had. I worked for an international delivery service, as a "Christmas Helper."

I would ride my bike to meet the truck in the morning, leave my bike all day, and get back to it in the evening after working ten or so hours. I could wax poetic for quite a while about all of the problems with that job, but the only real relation to the bike is that the job used up hours that I could have ridden, and that the bike is a part of the funny moment that I abruptly quit that horrible job.

From the moment that I came in contact with the delivery company, they had misrepresented things. I should have realized there would be problems when they weren't even honest to all of the applicants that showed up the day I did in order to apply for the coveted positions. They told all of us, in no uncertain terms, that no one would be hired on the day of the in-person application — but in fact, I and many others were.

And the lies just continued.

"You'll be paid for *this*." We weren't.

"Your hours will include all of *that*." They didn't.

And on and on.

Finally, one day, I had had enough. After working for about eight hours straight, running sprints to drop off packages, my driver told me that we were going to take a 15-minute break for lunch — and then work for another several hours.

I was fine with working the hours, but the game the drivers would play is that they would show us clocked out for at least an hour, rather than the 15 minutes. Unlike me, who was just doing this for a few bucks prior to school starting, the driver was in a competition for a permanent position, and the winners would be those who could show they could do the most work in the shortest period. It was to the driver's benefit to make it look like we had done 12 hours' work in 11 hours — and if doing so required me to be cheated out of an hour's pay, so be it.

I was tired of the dishonesty and cheating.

I looked at the driver and, with my arms pulling down imaginary handles from above my head, I said, "Do you know what this is?"

"No," he said.

"That's what a fighter pilot does to eject, when he needs to punch out...that's what I'm doing."

A little stunned, the driver said, "You mean you're not coming back tomorrow?"

"No," I said. "I mean I'm picking up my lunch box and helmet," as I pointed to their spots in the truck, "I'm walking the half mile to where my motorcycle is parked, and I'm leaving. See ya."

And with that, I did just that. I rode my bike back to my parents' house where we were staying temporarily, and was done with most of the riding I would do before law school.

***

The decision to switch from the University of Florida to Baylor came on soon, and then moving to Waco came not too long after that.

So, now I was back in a familiar town, but in an unfamiliar part of it. I would need to ride streets that I never, or at least rarely, rode while in Undergrad, in order to get to school every day. And in doing so, my propensity to exceed the speed limit would be a part of my daily commute.

***

Law School, particularly the first year, was beyond a full-time job. I got to school very early in the morning and stayed all day, studying when I was not in class. Then rode home, ate dinner, ran three miles, and then went back to the library to study until late in the evening.

Riding the miles home at night was not nearly as it would be years later, when I moved out in the country, because it was all small-city riding. There were plenty of street lights, and very light traffic.

The biggest thing about my riding during those days is that none of it was for fun. Or at least very little of it.

It was utilitarian. I rode because I needed to ride, so I didn't think much about it. By then, the bike had been my transportation for quite awhile.

I do, however, remember one very valuable lesson. And it's one that has no doubt saved my life since then.

At the time, after being in Waco a while, I had decided that I needed to be cool in the way the Marine Corps had not allowed. Obviously, there was no more orange vest. That item never resurfaced after the last day I rode on active duty.

Stupidly, though, I decided that I needed to be like all the cool guys riding around without helmets. I was still smart enough to always wear gloves and eye protection, and I'm pretty sure that I always wore jeans and boots, but feeling the breeze in my very short hair and just wearing a short-sleeved shirt, I had decided was a much cooler look. And after all, trying to look cool had always been a part of the purpose of riding a bike.

One sunny afternoon, when I didn't have a care in the world — other than making good grades — I came to an intersection on the ancient streets of Waco. Many of the streets there were crowned, so they forced an off-camber turn when going through them and making a left. And perhaps more importantly, Waco was not a wealthy city. Many of the vehicles driving around the streets of Waco were what I would later learn to call "Hoopties." They leaked. Oil and all kinds of other things were left deposited on the Waco roads, and of course, in the Waco intersections.

As I went through the intersection that day and made a left into the inside of the two lanes going in my intended direction, I opened up the throttle to power through the intersection and enjoy the feel. But suddenly — and I do mean suddenly — I was on my back, sliding across the pavement, through the other lane, and into the curb.

God protected me from anyone making a turn that would have put them in a position to run over me, and it is a miracle that my head did not smack the pavement, but it didn't.

The bike hit the curb, but not extremely hard, and I slid to a stop with a new lesson in hand — never give the bike gas in a turn, unless you are certain that you have the proper conditions to do it.

Just as I had gone down on the DT years earlier in the blink of an eye, I had done it here, and at higher speed — although thankfully not that much higher.

You would think that I would have learned my lesson that day. You would think that surely I now fully understood the importance of wearing a helmet, since any rider can hit the pavement — or worse — in an instant, and with no time to react. But I didn't. I continued to ride, daily, with no helmet, and no worries.

***

From way back in my motorcycle magazine-reading days as a teenager, I had always liked the look of the Enduro riders that one magazine showed. They had bandanas under their helmets, covering their mouths and noses. Given that I had grown up watching cowboy and western shows, it shouldn't have been a surprise that the desperado look is the one that caught my eye.

Accordingly, ever since my first bike, I had worn bandanas under my helmet on cold days, just as a way to keep a little warmer, and because I liked the look. But, that had always been when I was smart enough to wear a helmet.

The chin strap of the helmet helped the bandana stay in place at speed, and the helmet pretty much secured the whole situation.

Since my transportation riding had all been in Florida, Southern California, and Waco in the spring, summer, and fall, I had had very few times when the bandana look was needed. Now, however, winter was coming on, and though Waco has generally mild winters, it is not without at least a few very cold days. Also, without a heated seat, or hand grips, or anything, it didn't have to be that cold to feel pretty cold.

The Virago had no windshield, and I hated the look of them. But, hard times demand hard decisions, so I bought a cheap after-market detachable windshield, to see whether that would allow me to keep riding without a helmet.

It did for a few days, but then a cold snap hit.

That day demanded not just the jeans and boots and gloves, but also a long sleeve shirt, a canvas jacket, and the bandana — which then, in my mind, necessitated the helmet.

When I did wear a helmet, I had been smart enough to be riding with a full-face Arai helmet, back before anyone had ever heard of Arai. I originally bought it in San Diego, because it was the least expensive, decently rated helmet that I could find.

On that cold day, with the helmet and gear on, everything went fine on the morning ride over to school. There was no ice or noticeable precipitation on the streets, so it was pretty much like normal — just colder.

The ride back that day had me thinking about a number of things, and even that may have played a part in helping me. For the first time that I could remember, I was actually going at or under the speed limit, as I rode on the four-lane, one-way street, headed for home.

I was now in my fourth quarter, so I did not need to stay in the library every available minute that I was out of class. Because of that, it was not dark or at rush hour as I rode along.

The new windshield was uncomfortable to ride with, but not in a physical sense. It seemed to cause me to view the road in a different way which is hard to describe, but it was not good.

As I rode over the bridge above the train tracks and headed for the next of many intersections, I suddenly saw the truck. A large, paneled truck had decided to make a left-hand turn, from the far right lane.

I can't say that he took up all four lanes at once, because that seems physically impossible. But he was completely blocking my lane and any escape route, and in a split second, I grabbed all the brake I could and made impact.

***

As motorcycle wrecks on the street go, I almost couldn't have been any luckier. The truck that I collided with was paneled in that it was built in a similar fashion to the delivery trucks that I had ridden in a year or so earlier. Because of its height, I did not go over the top of the truck, but instead flew right into the side of it, like hitting a wall.

Fortunately, this wall was not built with I-beams, and instead had some "give" to it. The best description I can provide is that I hit and bounced off. The hitting wasn't good, and the bouncing off was fine, but the next contact was with the street — and it, of course, had zero "give."

As I lay in the middle of the street, with my bike on top of me, I couldn't move either leg or my right arm. As I understand it, the lack of movement was some sort of temporary paralysis, I guess caused by a shock to the system. The real concern at that point, though, was the shock to my other, more important muscles — the ones used to breathe.

I lay there in the street, in some sense gasping for air, and trying to get my bike off of me. My most vivid memory is of the traffic mostly just driving around me and going on about their day.

Fortunately, one of my classmates happened to be driving by. He stopped and came over to me and checked to see if there was anything that he could do. There wasn't much, and in those days very few people had a mobile phone, so I'm not sure how the ambulance was called, except that it was.

As with any wreck like this, the EMS guys didn't want to remove my helmet for fear of causing some spinal injury, and I will never forget laying in the back of the ambulance, with the oxygen mask taped on the outside of my full-face helmet, as if to simply tease me about the fact that I felt like I was about to die from lack of oxygen.

The ambulance got to the hospital, and they pulled the gurney out with me on it, and rushed me inside. As they did, some medical person got in my face and asked if I was allergic to anything, and I said, "Yes, not breathing."

Though I had been to an ER countless times by that point in my life, I don't think I had ever had as much pain as I did that day and for the next couple.

Unbelievably, I had not broken anything, according to the doctors, but everything hurt substantially, regardless.

I swore to my wife that I was done with motorcycles — at least street bikes. I would never ride another bike on the street, ever again.

If a collision this mild could cause this much pain, I didn't want to find out what one at speed would cause. I was done.

And then some time passed.

CHAPTER SIX

THE ROCKET BIKE

The wreck happened in November or December of 1988, and fortunately, it did not disrupt my schooling too badly. I recall having to attend class with some sort of bandage, I think, although I cannot imagine why. I may have missed a day or two of class — which is not good to do in law school — but it could have been so much worse.

My commitment to never riding another street bike was firm. When I replaced my bike so that I would have some transportation to and from school, I replaced it with a small pickup truck.

We were living off a student budget, so the truck we got was nothing fancy, and I'm sure that it had next to no safety features, other than seat belts, but at least driving it into the side of a truck, or anything else, wouldn't do what driving the bike into one did.

My bike had been "totaled," which, when you really look into it from a legal standpoint is a strange concept. Some people think that it means "the damage is more than it's worth," but that's not exactly correct. The full definition is something along the lines of: The cost to repair the vehicle, in its current condition is more than a reasonable person would pay to repair this particular vehicle, given the totality of the circumstances.

But who cared what the definition was? The bike was done. It was bent here and there and had a few things broken on it, but overall, it didn't look that bad. It had been a mild wreck — I just didn't want to have another one.

The months passed and winter turned to spring, which meant that I would be finishing up my fifth quarter at the end of the "normal" school year. That was significant, because given the way I was going through school — having started in a Spring Quarter — the normal thing to do in those days was go five quarters straight, take the summer off to Clerk, then do four quarters straight and graduate.

I had been very blessed in my schooling, and had done well. In fact, based on my resume and grades, I had my choice of any clerkship I wanted. And I wanted Dallas.

I had fallen in love with Dallas back in the late 1970s, as a Freshman at Baylor Undergrad. At that time, Dallas was magical. It was sparkling and new feeling and the city was run well.

I knew going into law school that I wanted to live in Dallas after I graduated, so Dallas firms were the only ones I considered for clerkship.

The normal way to do it was to clerk at two different firms — six weeks each — and then hopefully do a good enough job at each that you would have your choice of at least those two firms after law school.

I chose the biggest and best firm in Dallas at the time, which was named Johnson & Swanson. It was the place to be, and it paid the most of any of the firms. For my second choice, I wanted something different and chose a firm that was much smaller, but based on its client base was able to pay comparable salaries to Johnson & Swanson.

What all that meant was that I would be making good money that summer. Actually, really good money.

The smart thing to do would have been to save every cent of that money, and put it into the house that we would be needing the next year when I graduated. But as everyone knows, riding motorcycles is not about doing the smart thing.

***

In high school, with the DT and the Orange Junk Pile, I used a riding style that I love to this day. I don't know what other people call it, but for lack of a better term, I call it "up and down" — as in I'm sitting straight up and down.

In the Marines and law school, thus far, I had enjoyed the Cruiser style of riding. It was and is a posture that I felt and feel comfortable in on a bike, most of the time.

For some reason, though, in the summer of '89, I became fascinated with Sport Touring bikes. In looking back, I think that may have been the beginning of my desire to find Adventure through motorcycle *travel*, rather than just local exploring.

Adventure Bikes, as they are currently thought of, were not around yet — or at least not around anywhere that I was looking. But I still read motorcycle magazines as often as I could, and paid attention to the motorcycle world, at least to some extent.

Well, to be fair, it must have been more than to some extent, because I became fixated on the idea of owning a Sport Touring bike.

I never had much interest in owning what I consider to be a "pure sport bike" — and by that, I mean the street version of what the Moto GP riders ride. Although I went too fast when I drove or rode, typically, it was not the kind of crazy speeding that many people do on pure sport bikes. Or I guess I should say it was rarely that type.

I pushed the limits to some extent, but I never had the Top Gun "Need for Speed." Yes, the sport bikes were popular, and obviously even more so in those years due to Tom Cruise riding one in Top Gun, but that didn't matter to me. Riding was never about conformity and being part of the crowd — not even the motorcycling crowd.

Riding was always about fulfilling my dreams and having the adventures that I wanted to have. And now, sport touring was one of those adventures. The riding style looked like one I would enjoy, and the ability to carry luggage, go long distances, and go the speeds I would need to on trips seemed to be for me.

I was still convinced that Yamaha was the answer, almost regardless of the question. In fact, I don't even know if I considered any other make of sport tourer. Yamahas had proven themselves reliable to me, and I knew that they were good bikes. Actually, make that great bikes.

I don't recall where I was first introduced to it, but somewhere that summer, or just prior, I was introduced to the FJ 1200. This was, as I understood it, Yamaha's prize sport touring model. It was big, fast, and beautiful. And I decided that I wanted one — and now I had the money to do it.

And regarding that promise that I was finished with Street Bikes? That was made in haste, and it was just a promise to myself. I would just have to be more careful. I would just have to not wreck again. I would just have to whatever whatever. The FJ was beautiful, and the idea of living another day without a bike was more than I could take.

So now it was a quest.

***

Saying that I had the money meant that I had some money. Yes, I was paid well that summer, but Uncle Sam took a healthy cut of it. On top of that, we were maintaining two residences, since I was up in Dallas clerking, and my wife was in Waco during the week, and came up on the weekends.

All of that meant that I had a few thousand that I could afford
to spend on a toy. Or probably more to the point, wanted to spend
on a toy. And I began looking for well-maintained used FJs.

Given the experience I had had with the Orange Trash Heap
years earlier, though, I did not look at dealerships, since I did not
trust their honesty *vis-à-vis* used bikes. I looked in the Motorcycle
Trader magazine, or similar things, since the internet had not yet
arrived.

I found a gorgeous one. I don't remember the year, but I think
it was about a 1985 model. It was red and white and had very few
miles on it, and it was soon to be all mine.

I bought the bike and kept it at a friend's house, so that it could
live indoors, rather than outside at the apartment I was in that
summer. And right off the bat, I realized that something was very
different.

I had never noticed any real adjustment period in going from the
Up and Down to the Cruiser style, but this Sport Touring style
was very different.

At 6'2" in height and with generally poor flexibility, I found the
position to be somewhere between awkward and uncomfortable,
most of the time. So, my first adventure on the sport tourer would
be in a parking lot, trying to learn the nuances of how to make
turns and perform emergency maneuvers.

The reality is that I don't think I ever became what I would call
proficient at riding the beast.

I had some fun with it, but the real adventure to it — at least
it seemed to me — was living through riding it. I always felt like I

was hanging onto a rocket. It was a rocket that I controlled to some extent, but not completely. It felt like the bike was in charge, and it was just allowing me along for the ride, if I hung on.

According to the articles, the rocket could go 0-60 in 2.9 seconds, which made even our 5.0 Liter Mustang seem slow by comparison. More impressive, or frightening, than the 0-60, though was the roll-on speed.

I vividly recall going 40ish on the freeway on-ramp and after checking the blind spot, hitting the throttle to get up to freeway speed. In the blink of an eye, the rocket and I would go from 40 to 80 or 90. It felt instantaneous, and crazy.

In the motorcycling world, I liked cruising and gliding around on motorcycles much more than I liked being part of something that felt like it was part of a NASA experiment. In my mind, at least, this bike was just not made for cruising gently from one spot on the planet to another. It was made to get you from where you were to where you were going, fast. Very fast.

***

I don't know how many miles I put on the Red and White Rocket, but it couldn't have been too many. I did have some fun on it, and rode it to some interesting places around Waco, but never on that sport touring adventure that I had fantasized about.

The school year was flying by, I was headed for graduation, and I did not have much time to ride just for fun, even if I wanted to. More importantly, my first child was now on the way. We would be moving and buying our first home, and that extra money that was used for the toy was going to be needed to get our new life off the ground. And besides, I couldn't get killed at this point; I had too much on my plate and had to be responsible for my expected son.

The FJ never panned out to be what I had dreamed about. I still loved the look, but the reality, for me, did not match.

The FJ was sold to a guy who was huge and when he climbed on, to ride it off, he didn't look nearly as cool as I hoped I had while on it. But regardless, there it went, and with it, my riding days.

I was done.

CHAPTER SEVEN

DOING WITHOUT

I chose Johnson & Swanson as the law firm that I would begin my career with. They were right in Downtown Dallas, close to the courthouses, and they had prestige and the reputation for being the best firm in Dallas.

Everybody there was a heavy hitter, top of the class kind of a person, and a large part of their reputation for being the best was that nobody was going to out work us. For a first-year lawyer, assigned to the top team of litigators at the top firm, what that meant was unbelievable hours. All the top firms were known to be "sweatshops," and Johnson & Swanson was for sure — particularly the team of litigators that I was now the newest member of.

I worked just about every day that first year, except Christmas Day and Thanksgiving Day. I'm sure it wasn't truly every day, but it was awfully close. I vividly remember not coming in one Sunday, because I had nothing in particular that I had been assigned.

Shortly after church, I received a call at home asking why I wasn't in the office, and making it clear that I needed to be asap.

We wore suits every day, with ties, and worked ridiculous hours — often leaving to head home at 9:00 p.m., 11:00 p.m., Midnight, or 2:00 a.m. and beyond. I worked once from 8:00 a.m. on a Tuesday until 6:00 p.m. on a Thursday, with just 3 hours off on Wednesday to drive home, nap for 30 minutes, shower and return.

The drive, the hours, the attire, the totality of the circumstance just would not have lent itself to motorcycling. And besides, with the new baby at home, I had responsibilities.

During those first couple of years out of law school, I'm not sure that I even thought about motorcycles. They were a thing of the past, or so it seemed. But as my son got older, I started realizing that I wanted him to have everything in life that I had not been able to have.

On the feelings side of things, I never wanted him to feel the angst I had over not having the coolest thing around — and in my mind, of course that meant a motorcycle. Additionally, there was the practical side of things.

A fraternity kid at Baylor had gotten killed sometime around the time I was in law school or just before I started. He was younger than me and I didn't know him, but I knew a little about what happened, or was reported to have happened.

Apparently, he had taken a Baylor girl for a ride on a bike that he had borrowed. From what I had been told, he was somewhat of a novice rider. As it was explained to me, a fatal decision was made to make a U-Turn on an undivided highway, and when he did, he allegedly pulled right in front of a fast-moving car or truck. The thought of it was brutal.

Motorcycle deaths happen all the time, but my understanding of this one was that it could have been avoided with better training and more experience. Without regard to whether that was true, I projected ahead in my mind to my son growing up, and being in a position like I was in college, to borrow someone's bike, "just to have some fun."

Just like I would never let him grow up not knowing how to swim and stay alive in and around water, I wanted him to know how to ride. If he chose not to later, all the better, since riding for me is like anything else dangerous I've done. I did it because I wanted to, but I wanted my son to stay as safe as possible.

As they say, kids grow up way too fast. Before long, he was big enough, and it was time. Time for that first motorcycle.

***

I think he was about nine at the time. And unfortunately, by the time he got to that age, I was divorced. What that meant was that I didn't have the financial freedom to just go buy him the top of the line, or at least I felt like I didn't. So, I was back in the used bike market.

I still trusted Yamaha, and ended up getting him an 80cc bike, very similar to what I wanted when I was just a little older than he was. If he wanted to learn to ride in the dirt like I had always wanted to learn more about, I wanted him to have the chance.

Riding in the dirt where we lived, though, meant riding in big fields. The fields were mostly grass-covered, and some of the grass was very tall.

I don't remember that I was able to give him a lot of opportunities, but at least he learned to ride, and I could live adventures vicariously by watching him. His little sister was too young at that time, but whenever I had them both, I needed to watch them both, so the riding that my son got to do wasn't too much more than what my neighbor had done in Georgia — an oval on flat ground. Nevertheless, I would have given anything to have even these few, small opportunities at that age.

As he grew, my son liked riding his bike some. But I don't think he liked it as much as I liked seeing him do it. I know I tried to give him an opportunity once in what would have been his most adventurous off road situation, but it never panned out to be what I hoped for. The planned ride was on a limited course and had a great many trees. In addition to that, the used bike's reliability issues brought on additional problems. His first bike turned out to be about like mine had been — just a place to begin.

***

Time passed, the 80cc bike sat more than it was ridden, and before I knew it, my son was 12. By that time, he had outgrown the 80, and it was a pain anyway. It was time for the next chapter, both of life and of his motorcycling. So, I decided the Honda 100 Enduro model would be the next move. I don't recall what the letters were at that time, but I think it was an XR 100. It was sweet.

His little sister had a pink Barbie jeep that ran on batteries, and I would load it and the Honda up and take the kids up to the fields to ride and drive when I could. There, to my almost horror, I learned a valuable lesson about off-road riding. Never assume what you can't see.

I did not know that lesson, so I had not taught it to my son, and he could have gotten seriously hurt, due to my ignorance.

Given their ages, I felt like I needed to keep a much closer eye on my daughter, when we were all up at the giant field. She wasn't close to traffic or any specific danger, but the little jeep was mobile, and given some time, she could have driven herself into some danger.

My son, on the other hand, was just riding big circles and figure 8s and things like that, out in the tall grass of the enormous area.

We were in a part of the DFW Metroplex where new homes and apartments had been being built for a decade or a little longer, but there were still a great many wide open areas. I had never understood the importance of the "No Dumping" signs, until that day.

As I was watching my daughter, I would periodically look up to see my son. I don't know what he was thinking about, but I imagine that he was in some imaginary race, going as fast as he felt like he could, and then making the turn to come back in the other direction. Everything was fine, until I looked up, and he wasn't there. He was nowhere to be seen.

I couldn't figure out where he could have gone, but he popped up pretty shortly after I saw he wasn't there. He had hit something — something hard.

Some construction crew, who knows how many months or years earlier, had decided that they would take advantage of a large empty lot, and no one to stop them. They decided that the middle of this big field would be a good spot to dump what was probably at least a couple hundred pounds of concrete. And there it lay, not bothering anyone, hidden by all the tall grass, until my son hit it at a speed that could have injured him badly or worse.

I, stupidly, had not even thought to check the area, or walk the layout of his makeshift track or even to tell him to drive it slowly and carefully first, before taking it at speed. I just assumed that tall grass meant tall grass, and that the only thing "in" the grass was more grass.

Looking back, that was idiotic. There could have been rebar, broken glass, or anything hidden in the grass. And in retrospect, my son was fortunate that all that happened to him was a scare and a bent front wheel.

***

In the next year or so, my daughter got old enough that I thought she needed to ride, also. It's not that she had expressed some big interest in it, but I didn't want her to end up on a bike later in life and get hurt, if I could avoid it by making sure that she knew how to ride.

Now, with both of them riding, and having gone years without a bike, I decided that it was time for me to start riding again.

I found a used XR 600 that was just what I needed — I thought. We all had Hondas and we could all go ride together, just like in all of those brochures that show the happy families doing that. One of the problems, though, was that it's somewhat difficult to have multiple levels of adventure all at the same time.

My daughter could ride competently, but just in big flat circles; my son could do a little better than that, and then there was me. I am not sure that I could have done much more. I certainly had never learned all those motocross skills that I dreamed about as a child and teen. But, at least now I had a bike that could do some things that I had never experienced.

The front wheel of that big XR could come up with just a slight twist of the wrist. I had never done wheelies on a bike before, because I hadn't had a bike that could, or at least nothing like this. It was fun experimenting with the XR, and looking back on it, I wish I had taken advantage of it and used it to gain better dirt skills. I am not sure how I could have, other than just trial and error, but back then I was young enough that getting a little banged up with it while learning wouldn't have been such a serious concern.

But then my life took other turns with relationships and such, and the bikes mostly stayed in the storage facility, not being ridden nearly as much as they should have.

As my life took one more big turn, it was time for a new kind of biking adventure.

Chapter Eight

THE HARLEY YEARS

I had never been a Harley guy. In fact, I hadn't even thought about them much.

Probably the closest I ever came to one was in the Safety Course that the Marine Corps mandated. One of the troops that was taking the class had a Harley. It was fairly small, so my guess is that it was a Sportster, or whatever the entry-level Harley was in about 1985.

Frankly, there was nothing about that Marine's Harley that impressed me. It seemed a little like the odd machine out, among all of the Japanese bikes that all the rest of us in the class had. After the two-day course, I never saw that Harley again, and don't think I thought about them until about 15 years later.

Looking back, I don't even know how I decided Harleys were the next chapter in my life. I just knew that I needed to get back to street bikes. I had been without the FJ or any other street bike now for a little over a decade, and it was time.

Fortunately, Harleys were becoming a big thing at that time — 2001. They seemed to be showing up everywhere. And so did their dealerships. There was one right by my house now. So I went in, not even knowing one Harley from another.

***

The bike that caught my eye was one of the smallest they had. It was a Sportster 883 Custom.

I had been looking at biking magazines and liked the look of the drag bars on a sleek bike, and that's what this Bronze 883 Custom was. It was beautiful, and the fact that it was a bike that would turn out to be much smaller than what I needed never occurred to me.

I wanted something that I could buy for cash immediately, so I didn't even look at the bigger bikes that day. To be honest, they probably intimidated me, after not riding a street bike for so long, not riding a cruiser since the collision in 1988, and never even being on a bike as massive and heavy as the Softails and other models looked to be.

The 883 became mine, immediately. And with that purchase, I became part of what I hoped would be a family that looked for adventures on bikes.

I was now single, and the bike would be an easy adventure date. It would certainly weed out any women who did not at least tolerate an interest in bikes.

I think that I had only owned the bike for a matter of a few hours when I took a date on a ride for the first time.

Getting back on the road after all those years was an adventure unto itself. The person I was taking on the ride lived on the other side of Dallas – Fort Worth from me, and that is a long way. Riding over there put me on busier roads that I had probably ever been on, and at a time when the word "rusty" would have been a gross understatement.

I don't think we rode very far on our date — just to a restaurant and back — but then came the ride back home late at night on the new bike. And that, of course, brought another layer to the adventure.

With atrophied skills, on roads that can be crazy in broad daylight and get much crazier late at night, I rode and prayed and eventually made it back home safely.

After that first ride, I was able to just get out and relearn all of the things that I needed to know in order to have enjoyable and safe rides. As the saying goes about bicycles, once you learn, allegedly you never forget.

What I found to be truer with motorcycles is that once you learn, you never forget the basics. The nuances, however, take a while to come back. And often, the nuances are what can keep you alive.

Over a relatively short period of time, I remembered all of the safety tips that I had pored over and tried to practice. Lane positioning, looking for outs, using cars to block for me through intersections — all of those things came back with time. What seemed to be equally valuable, though, was what Harley was famous for bringing to the table — sound. The 883 sounded awesome. It was loud without being obnoxious, and anyone around me in traffic would almost certainly know that I was there. That alone seemed like it would help stop people swerving into my lane, if I did make the mistake of ending up in their blind spot.

I'm pretty sure that up to a certain point, early in my 883 days, I went back to the discipline that I had had from my youth of always wearing a helmet.

I certainly wanted to look cool. What was the point in riding a bike if that was not at least one of your goals? And so many people were riding without helmets or with the kind that appeared to be little more than decorations — and they all looked cool — so I know that I experimented with no helmet and the decoration variety. Nevertheless, I think I was pretty good about maintaining some sense about the value of a helmet.

And then I was influenced, for the worse.

It was another ride date, and I wore my helmet and brought one for her. This was a first date, so of course I didn't want to say the wrong thing, or do anything offensive.

As I recall, she had told me that she had been on a motorcycle a number of times in the past, so when I arrived, I recall that one of our first topics was what we would wear as we rode. I didn't want to assume anything so I asked, "Do you want to wear helmets?"

She responded, "What do you usually do?"

"Sometimes I do, and sometimes I don't," I said, trying to keep all of my bases covered.

As if she knew just how to say it, and with a cute Texas Tech twang, the response came after a brief pause, "Oh...sometimes I don't."

And the message was clear. Don't be a dweeb. Be cool. Ride without a helmet.

So off we went, and it was great.

***

I know that the 883 took me on many other adventures, quite a few of which were date rides, but only one other is particularly memorable. And the memories of it come from the lesson it taught me, and how it changed my thinking about what needed to be a part of my future adventures.

It was another first date, so of course in addition to looking my best, I needed my bike to. Going back to my days with the DT, I always prided myself on how sharp my bikes looked. The wash and wax of course never took long, because even big bikes can be covered in no time.

In addition to that, though, I also wanted all of the leather and other parts that don't get waxed to look their best. Somewhere in life, someone had introduced me to Armor All. Since I wasn't a MotoGP Rider and didn't lean far into my turns, I always felt like it was safe for me to at least apply Armor All to the sides of the tires, and since I had very few passengers up until this time, I would always apply Armor All to the seat. It would look sharp, and I never noticed the slipperiness too much as I rode. The only other bike that I had ever had with passengers to any extent was the Virago, and it had a backrest, so I never worried or even thought about Armor All *vis-à-vis* a passenger.

The 883 was different. Part of the sleek look was the seat. The passenger portion of the seat was small and almost pointed to the back of the bike as though it were an available exit. Still, I never even thought about it when preparing the bike for the night's activities. So, Armor All it was — it had to look perfect.

When I arrived, the bike did look perfect. But I will never forget the first time she saw it.

"Oh, I thought you had a *big Harley*," or words to that effect. I would have preferred that she punch me in the gut.

It had never occurred to me that the 883 was seen as a sort of "little brother" to the other Harleys. But apparently, it was. And now, having been told that, in so many words, I couldn't unhear it or unthink it.

Regardless, the 883 is what we had for that night's ride. So, off we went.

The first part of the date was unmemorable. I'm sure we went to some burger joint or something, and then some other activity — who knows what. But then it was getting later, and neither of us wanted the date to end.

"What should we do now?" I asked

"Well...I have been wanting to get my piercing re-done," she said.

I tried not to look stunned. I had never had a date say that or anything like it before — let alone as a proposal for the night's activities on a first date — but...okay.

"Do you know somewhere you want to go?"

"Yes," she said, "I know a place on the other side of Fort Worth."

By now, it was probably about 11:30 p.m., and the ride would be quite a few miles, on a freeway for about 30 or 40 minutes.

"Let's go." And we hopped on the 883 and took off.

The ride over was uneventful, other than I'm sure I was thinking, "This ought to be interesting." And we made it to the place — a tattoo and piercing shop that looked about like any other I had ever seen from the outside.

During my time in the Marine Corps, I had seen quite a few tattoos, but I didn't have any. The years I was on active duty were before the time when it seemed everyone in society had tattoos, and at that time at least, Officers were not supposed to have tattoos. The exception to the rule was the Officers that had been prior enlisted. They could have them, assuming they had gotten them while Enlisted. As with a lot of things during that time, I'm not sure that it was an actual regulation; it just seemed to be the way it was.

Since neither I nor any of my friends got tattoos during my Marine Corps days, and none of the lawyers that I knew — or even law students — had tattoos that I can remember, I had never been in a tattoo shop, at least as far as I can remember. It was an interesting place, and all the more so past midnight on a Friday or Saturday night.

The characters in the shop were just what you would hope for. They were straight out of Central Casting, and I wouldn't have wanted the experience to be any different.

My date knew what she was doing, because as she had said, she was getting something "re-done." It was not her first rodeo.

I found my spot to observe the procedure, since she wanted me there.

Then it hit me.

My lack of understanding of the ins and outs of tattoos was nothing compared to my ignorance of the piercing world. I knew people got them. I saw people with them. I thought they often looked horrible, and had no interest in ever getting one. And I had never thought about the process much, so this was the first time it occurred to me.

The guy who's about to stick this painful-looking implement into this person is not a medical professional.

We're not talking about a needle. This seemed to me to be the equivalent of an ice pick, or worse. The guy was holding a very sharp poking type implement, and he was about to stab her with it, and not only was this guy clearly not an M.D., there was not one in sight.

In particular, I thought, it would be nice to have maybe an anesthesiologist nearby.

By this time, she was past the point of no return. The stabbing happened. Suddenly, the thought of the whole thing looked like it had gone well past the fun stage for my date. She was now in pain, really severe pain.

I'm pretty sure that as the pain hit, she wished she could have changed her mind. But now, the jab was done, the pain was there, and it was getting worse. And we had the ride home yet to do.

I don't know when, exactly, the pain went from severe pain to absolute agony, but it did. It was somewhere along our ride, because we left right after the bloodshed. She encouraged me to ride as fast as I could, and I did ride as fast as I dared.

By now, it was 1:30 a.m. or so and we were screaming — if not literally, at least figuratively — across the freeways, trying to get her home. And it would have been a great time for a backrest that she could have to some extent relaxed into.

Instead, what she had was a very tiny, very slippery seat — that was built in such a way that it would help you make an unwanted exit, even if it wasn't as slick as greased lightning, and we weren't going 80+ mph, and she wasn't trying to hold on for dear life.

I have had a great many motorcycle rides in my five decades plus of riding, but I am not sure that any were crazier than this one. It was an adventure of another kind.

***

Not too long after the Piercing Adventure, I decided that I did indeed need to part with my beautiful little friend — my first Harley. The 883 would need to go, so that I could get a "proper" Harley. I needed one that would allow for no derision.

But I had not had the 883 that long. It was essentially still brand new, and I had not learned all about the different types of Harleys.

As always, though, God was looking out for me. Not knowing any different, I went by looks for the most part, I thought all of the

Harleys in the dealership were beautiful, but some more so than others.

I particularly loved the look and name of the Fatboy. This being about 2002, the Fatboys were not as fat as they would get in later years, but the solid wheels made a bold statement, and getting on the bike felt like climbing into a recliner. It was awesome.

Then I learned something new. The fear that I had had for years about bigger bikes was, at least with respect to Fatboys, completely unwarranted. This bike — weighing somewhere around 700 pounds, without me on it — felt like it was a part of me.

The center of gravity was so low, and the bike so well built that the Fatboy was easier to ride than the 883 or Virago had been. And it was about a million times easier, more comfortable, and less stressful to ride than the FJ had been.

I was sold. I needed the Fatboy.

And then the monetary adventure of owning a "basic" Harley began.

The bike was beautiful as it came. It was red and silver two-tone, and looked nice. But I needed it to look better — and boy, does Harley have just what you need, or what you think you need.

In looking through their complimentary catalogue — a genius marketing move — it seemed that virtually everything on the bike, other than the tires, gas tank, and seat, could be replaced with chrome. And as for the parts of the bike that were already chrome, they have a deal for you there, too. You can replace those with better chrome pieces! Maybe there would be some design on it or it would be fancier or whatever, but the bottom line is that the new bike you just purchased could be reimagined and have a zillion different parts on it swapped out or added to it.

None of that is for free, of course. In fact, quite the opposite. And as for what to do with the replaced pieces, they would be happy to keep those, if you didn't remember to request them back.

Of course, it's not like requesting to keep the old parts gave you anything but some slight satisfaction that you were not enriching the shop any more than the thousands that you were already spending on the new parts were. It's not like there was much that could be done with old, stock handgrips or footpegs or whatever.

***

I'm not sure that I ever got everything that I wanted on the bike, but I added a lot. I know that I spent thousands on a variety of different pieces to get the bike as close as possible to exactly how I wanted it to look. And in addition to that, came the expenditures to get the bike to sound and feel the way I wanted it to sound and feel.

The shotgun pipes not only looked awesome, they had a sound that was music to the ears of anyone who likes the sound of bikes. They could be loud but were not obnoxious, and they had a soul-thumping roar.

It seemed though, that all the coolest bikes had ape hanger handlebars. At least that was my thought at the time.

With the 883, I realized that the cool look I liked of the drag bars just wasn't that comfortable to ride, and it certainly was not the look I needed for this new beast.

I don't recall the handlebars that the bike came with, and they were probably adequate, but if there was no other reason to get new handlebars, the fact that the stock ones were stock was probably enough for me.

So, along with some other chrome that I felt like I just couldn't live without, I decided to get new handlebars. And in doing so, I realized the importance of doing some research prior to walking into a high-priced dealership or shop with money burning a hole in your pocket.

Yes, I desperately wanted new handlebars. They needed to be better looking, and of course they would be expensive. Unfortunately, though, I had no idea what I wanted or how it all worked.

Did I want 10-inch bars? or 12-inch? or 16? or more?

Did I want internal wiring — inside of the handlebars — or keep the external? Had I even thought of the cost and options *vis-à-vis* the wiring, given that anyone should realize that stock wiring for 4 inch bars won't work with 18-inch Apes. I had never thought of that.

Did I want them set up or back or how? Et cetera, etc.

The other pieces were easier. They were just items out of the catalogue that I was adding onto the bike — at great expense.

I got the bike back from the shop after a few days. It looked better than it had, although I was not sure it had reached the look

I was going for. The extra chrome looked awesome. Included the bolted-on pieces around the rear axle.

I will never forget those overpriced axle pieces — because soon after that first ride out of the shop one of them became a paperweight.

Within 2 miles of the shop, after spending a couple thousand dollars or so on parts and labor, at least one piece of beautiful chrome fell off my bike, and was never seen again. The corresponding piece on the other side of the bike — the one that held firm — ended up being a paperweight from that point forward, since it's counterpart became trash on the side of the road.

And within a week or two, I realized that buying — and having installed at great expense — new handlebars, without knowing for sure that you are getting what you really want, is a costly mistake.

The old bars were gone, the new ones were not what I wanted, and all the new wiring would need to be replaced, when I finally got what I wanted a few months later.

***

With quite a bit of trial and error and cost, I eventually had a bike that I could be proud to ride, and that I enjoyed riding.

The Fatboy was an amazing ride; it felt like we were one. It always reminded me of the technology you see in science fiction movies and the actual military technology that responds based on where you look. It seemed like all I needed to do was think of where I wanted the bike to go, and it went — with great looks, sound, and comfort.

I had some enjoyable date rides on the bike, and none of the women who ever rode on the back ever complained again about my bike not being a "big" Harley. It was as perfect a bike as I had ever had.

I never could figure out the Harley family (HOG — Harley Owners' Group) completely, but I was able to have a couple of adventure rides with them, nonetheless.

One ride started at Midnight or so and we rode through the countryside for an hour or two as a group of maybe 30 or 40 bikes roaring along. Looking back now, and knowing what I now know of riding in the country at night — with animals loose everywhere — I'm not sure that it was the smartest ride in the world, but it was fun and memorable.

Another ride we did was from the DFW area up to Hot Springs, Arkansas. It was a fun ride, but it introduced me — maybe for the first time — to the reality that you need more than one thing in common with a group of people to really bond. At least I do.

Bikes alone are just not enough — even the same brand of bike.

The HOG group had people of all shapes and sizes, including a guy who, sadly, really was riding a bike that was way too big for him. He was probably about 5'5" tall and he was riding one of the biggest bikes that Harley made. As he tried to slow-ride his full dresser in a parking garage, in front of all of his HOG friends, he dropped it at least once, if not twice.

Everyone was nice, and the trip was okay, but it was also pretty boring. No one seemed to have anything to talk about except, "Hey, nice bike." "Thanks, yours too."

Every conversation on the ride ended about like the scene in Dumb and Dumber where Lloyd Christmas walks out of the 7-11 and comments on the Big Gulps — "Whelp, see ya later."

The ride was long enough that we had several stops, and I did get a chance to observe and try to learn more about long-distance riding — the adventure that I had long wanted to take. I got to see options for rain gear and helmets and windshields and riding position.

Ultimately, though, the most memorable part of this adventure ride was the ride home.

I had a new girlfriend, and really wanted to get back to see her on the night I had planned, so I broke off from the group early to head back.

It's not that the group and I were going to be going different routes back, it's that a storm was blowing in that any reasonable person would have waited out — especially given that we had reached the top of the DFW Metroplex.

While the others wisely found a place to hole up, I pressed on. It was the worst storm that I ever rode in, and in retrospect, I'm probably lucky to have made it through without a catastrophe.

The rain was absolutely pouring, and with it, of course came some wind. I was on the DFW freeways, and so were lots of people in cars.

At that time, I had a full face helmet that I had purchased, although I didn't always wear it. In this storm, I certainly did.

The sensation was surreal. In traffic, at high speeds, in pouring rain, and looking through the peephole of a face shield, it seemed that I was watching a television show that appeared to be showing some moron trying to die.

"Wow! That looked dangerous," I would think.

"Oh man! That was close."

It seemed that the guy in the show was taking his life in his hands.

Then every so often, it would occur to me that the guy in the show was me.

I had on reasonable gear to protect me from the pain of the rain — that needle sensation that you know if you've ridden in any — but nothing was rainproof, and it wouldn't have helped with the danger, anyway.

I made it home, with no events, and was glad I did. But after I was safe, I knew that I never wanted to ride in rain — particularly rain like that — ever again.

***

The Fatboy was a great bike. The adventures I had on it on the few HOG rides and the date-rides were incredibly enjoyable, memorable, or both. But as with any relationship between a man, his bike, and his latest girlfriend, eventually the girlfriend is no more, and it's back down to just the man and his bike. I was back to just the Fatboy and me.

I was in a girlfriend lull, but I had discovered a place to ride that seemed to exude adventure. It was a place called Strokers, and it was like a mini-Sturgis or Daytona Bike Week, every week.

Strokers was a restaurant, bar, outdoor concert area, custom bike shop, and bike show, all rolled into one. Every weekend, a huge crowd of bikes would descend on Strokers. There were bikes everywhere, live music, and plenty of people to watch and meet.

Among the hundreds there every weekend, there were everything from hardcore bikers to guys in khakis and boat shoes. Everyone just mingled and had the commonality of a love for bikes.

More importantly, for me, was the fact that there were people there with whom I shared more in common than just bikes. There was at least one, and maybe more, Motorcycle Clubs that were made up of former Marines. And the Brotherhood of the Marine Corps always gives plenty to talk about and reason to hang out — well almost always.

I met up with some Marines who all rode Harleys like me, and they were all in or joining the Leatherneck Motorcycle Club. That seemed like a good idea for me, too. With this group, I would have the opportunity to ride and not be stuck with just Big Gulp conversations at the breaks.

I joined the Club and began riding with the group.

On the first group ride that I attended, we rode out into the countryside. It takes a while to get there from the heart of the

Metroplex, but the way the leader of the group led, it was not too long.

65 mph....75 mph...85 mph...95 mph...105 mph... And there didn't seem to be an end in sight.

We were screaming down a small country road like our hair was on fire. At about 105, my tolerance for ridiculous speed was hit. I slowed and pulled over to the side allowing the rest of the group to continue on trying to break the land speed record. I didn't want any more of that type of riding.

After just a few minutes, I saw one of the group approaching, riding toward me in the opposite direction.

"Are you okay?"

"Yes," I assured him, "I'm just not interested in riding like that."

He got the message and passed it on as appropriate, and we were done with that level of recklessness, at least so long as I was there.

The better part of being in the group was getting to meet a couple of other Marines who I seemed to have more in common with, and with whom I could have the excitement that I was looking for.

The two best friends I made were great guys, former Marine Infantry, and current Firefighters. They both had Harleys similar to mine and both had riding styles that were close enough to mine that we rode well together.

We were all single and had plenty of free time to ride. They had Firemen schedules that would give them off a couple of days at a time, and I worked for myself, and could pretty much make the schedule that I wanted to, at least in the evenings and on weekends..

On many nights, I would head over to their place and listen as they fired up their bikes and let them warm up good and long. That wouldn't be so noteworthy except that one of the guys had taken whatever it is out of his pipes or engine that made the sound of his bike the noise that you would use if you were trying to traumatically destroy your hearing.

His bike was beautiful, but it was abusively loud. Or, I guess you could say, enjoyably loud, if you were in the group riding with him — unless you were directly behind him at a stoplight.

Some of the best memories I have on a motorcycle are tearing around the DFW Metroplex on our loud, beautiful Harleys at 2:00 a.m., 3:00 a.m., and beyond. The picture in my mind of us racing up and over the extremely large overpasses found in our area, heading from one bar to another, is one that I hope to never lose. Those times were the types of times that I wish I could have bottled and poured out again and again over the rest of my life.

But, like everything, those times came to an end. I met a new girlfriend who eventually became my wife; both of the guys got girlfriends and eventually wives; and the late-night Harley adventures just started living in my memories, apparently never to be relived.

***

Sherry was my new girlfriend and riding companion. And the fact that I found her, at least at first, worked well with my other love, motorcycles. She enjoyed riding with me, or pretended to.

We would ride sometimes with one of the other Marines and his girlfriend, or with a few other friends who had bikes.

Sherry and I both had small children, and of course should have been riding with helmets at all times, but didn't.

We had plenty of other protective gear — thick leather jackets, leather chaps, boots, gloves, eye protection, everything you would need. Except that we didn't want to mess up our cool with helmets.

Stupidly, we rode the freeways at high speeds, in groups and out, in heavy traffic and out, without helmets. We would do it late at night or anytime during the day.

And then it all almost came to an end.

We had been out riding with one or more of our friends, somewhere in and around the Metroplex that day, and we were headed home. We were on what was still labeled a Farm to Market Road, but what had grown up to be much more.

The speed limit was about 45 and there were plenty of cars around, but it was not overly stressful riding. As we headed for home, we only had about 3 or 4 more stop lights to go.

We were behind some sort of commercial vehicle — a truck of some kind. From memory, it looked to be a plumbing truck or electrical, or something like that. It was much bigger than a pickup, and seeing around it or over it was impossible.

We were a safe distance behind it and going the speed limit, approximately. Thank God that we were.

It was late afternoon, but not that late, and we were living the dream.

Suddenly, I realized that the truck was not moving. It was at a dead stop, with no brake lights working. And we were going to hit it going 45 or so, if I didn't do something fast.

At that time, Sherry was relaxed on the back and I was cruising and hanging onto the beautiful 18-inch ape hangers. Immediately, I grabbed all of the front and back brakes that I could get.

During my BMX days as a youth, we used to admire all of the big-name Motocross riders, and we particularly liked what we used to call "crossing it up." We could mimic the position by locking our brakes up, usually in the dirt, since our bicycles could never get enough speed to effect a cross-up on the street. Crossing it up, for us, was sliding sideways, with our bicycles perpendicular to the direction of travel.

Unlike our childhood bicycles, though, my Fatboy could definitely travel fast enough to slide on the street. And that's exactly what we did.

I have always been interested in other riders' stories about their wrecks or almost wrecks.

I have heard many a tale of "laying it down," and one guy even claimed that as he was headed for a collision, he "laid it down, and got up on top of it and rode it" — it being his Harley. Okay, maybe they did lay their's down, and maybe he did "ride" his. But I wasn't them.

I wouldn't know how to "lay" a bike down at speed, on purpose, if I wanted to. And I don't want to learn.

When I grabbed all the brake available, my 700-pound Harley with 200+ pounds of me and about 100 pounds of Sherry, re-lived my BMX days. We were sliding sideways towards the stopped truck, with the rear tire pretty much beside the front tire, and we weren't going to make it.

In a flash, I calculated that we were not going to stop in time. We were going to make impact, and it was going to be hard — possibly deadly.

I quickly glanced over my left shoulder and saw that no one was in the turn lane to our left, and made a snap decision that all those years of riding as a kid allowed me to make.

I let off the brakes, the rear tire popped back around to where it should be, I steered — or counter-steered, it all happened so fast, I'm not sure which — to the left about 15 feet, and then grabbed brake again, but not as hard.

We came to a stop at the light, right beside the truck and driver that had almost ended our lives.

I was shaking with fear about what almost happened.

The light turned green and we slowly made a left and then a right into the pharmacy parking lot that happened to be right there. I pulled the bike to a spot out of the way, and sat there, thanking God that I had not just killed us both, or worse.

I don't recall if I turned the bike off or how long we sat there, but it took me a while to lose the feeling of what had just happened and almost happened. Eventually, the immediacy of the feeling passed, and we headed for home — on back roads and at very slow speeds.

I had never wanted to find out how the Fatboy would handle under emergency conditions, but now I knew. It was amazing.

The low center of gravity, the apes, the braking — it all worked to perfection.

We were blessed that I had had the experiences that I had had growing up, and that I had read all of those articles and thought so much about lane position and always looking for an "out." But ultimately, we were blessed that God had spared us and that we both didn't end up in the ICU or morgue.

***

Like every other motorcycling chapter of my life, eventually, the Fatboy chapter would have to end as well.

Sherry and I continued riding after the close call, and we had one or two other close calls that weren't quite as dramatic, but none of those caused us to stop riding.

Instead, as with the FJ, it was eventually a new baby that would spell the end of all of the adventures that the Fatboy would have with us. We found out that our first son was on the way, and that nagging call of responsibility began to sound in my psyche.

The bike got parked in the garage, with no plan to get rid of it. We just knew that we weren't going to ride it together — sadly, probably, ever again.

Like an old family dog that is replaced by a child, the Fatboy got moved to the side, figuratively and I guess really literally. I would take it out and half-heartedly ride every once in a while, to "give it some exercise." But we had no extended family to take care of our new child, if something happened. And the risk just wasn't worth the reward — at least it didn't seem to be.

At some point, I just couldn't bear to see the dust continue to collect on the beautiful old friend and companion, and we made the decision to let it go to a new home.

No one ever takes care of your baby as well as you do, and watching your motorcycle ride off, in the hands of a new owner, is one of the saddest feelings in motorcycling.

CHAPTER NINE

BACK IN THE GAME

Our first son arrived — Zach, and he seemed to be a lot like me. He loved the toy motorcycles that I kept in my office for when he would visit, and liked his little electric trike that he could ride, like it was a motorcycle.

I'm not sure exactly when the Fatboy went to its new home, but Zach had to be around three years old. Of course, what that meant in my mind was that in just a couple of years or so, I would be wanting to teach him how to ride — assuming that he wanted to learn.

On his 5th or 6th birthday, it was time to begin.

Zach got the brand new Honda CRF 50 that I had dreamed about having when I was a few years older than him. I made sure to get him all of the safety gear that I could find and had located a safe place for him to learn to ride.

We lived in a congested neighborhood, but fortunately the part of the Metroplex that we lived in still had some open spaces that were unfenced. More importantly, they did not have "No Trespassing" signs on them.

At some time in my life, I had heard Evel Knievel talk about how his father had taught him to ride — or maybe it was how he taught his kids to. Either way, it made great sense to me, particularly given what had happened to me on my first ride.

The description was that the best thing to do was to tie a rope around the rider's waist, and then have him or her ride in a circle around Dad.

If, as had happened to me, there was a brain malfunction or rider freeze-up or even a mechanical malfunction, the rider could be pulled off of the bike before it got up to high speed or anything else horrific happened.

So that's what we did, in a big field that would become a huge shopping center and grocery store, within about a year of that time.

Zach rode a few times in that lot, but soon thereafter, we decided to move to an adventure park of our own.

***

In 2013, we moved from the congested neighborhood to a five-acre ranch in the heart of the Metroplex. We bought it in large part for Sherry's horses, but also so that Zach and his little brother Jackson could have a place to run and play and do all of the things that I wanted to do as a boy.

There was room for archery, horseback riding, BB guns, baseball, football, and motorcycles.

The horses could be put up in the barn and virtually the entire five-acre spread could be turned into a mini-bike track. Yes, you needed to be extra careful going through the steel pipe fencing, but there were enough extra-wide or double-wide gates that even that did not make for too much concern.

And getting to watch Zach ride was great fun. Obviously, though, that could only go on so long. Within a few months of moving, I had to have another bike, and this time, it was back to my roots.

Honda made a CRF 250 that seemed to be exactly what I needed to ride around with Zach and his 50. Better yet, Jackson had turned five, and it was time for him to learn to ride too.

So now we had two CRF 50s and a CRF 250 and five acres upon which to have fun. What more could we ask for?

We would open the gates and engage in pretend races. We tried to build little jumps here and there, but not much came of them.

I certainly had never learned how to do much in terms of dirt track riding, so there was only so much that I could teach the boys, but I could try.

In addition to the fun we had, there was peace of mind. I wanted all of my kids to learn to ride, in part, hoping that they would "get it out of their system."

Although I would never want to talk any of the children out of their dreams or something that was truly in their blood, I also did not want to encourage them to ride street bikes.

After the experience I had had hitting the pavement and almost worse, I was well aware of how dangerous it could be. At one point, I had three friends or friends of friends get killed on bikes within one year.

One of my good friend's sons — a young man that I loved like a son and was one of the finest young men I knew — died tragically one night on a dark road on a bike.

I wanted to do what I could to avoid that with my kids, all while also allowing them to learn some valuable skills and having some fun and adventure.

Of course the same rules didn't apply to me. I wanted to ride, and by the time I had the CRF 250 with me at our small ranch for a while, it had been several years since I had ridden on the road for anything other than going to get some gas. I needed to have something that would allow me to at least ride on the road a little bit.

And I had been noticing in my motorcycle travel magazines that there were now these bigger on-off bikes like what I had grown up with. I didn't really get it, and didn't understand the point of them, but I was seeing really large "Enduro" bikes and they seemed to be gaining in popularity.

***

I guess it's possible that the large on-offs had been a thing for years. I do recall that even as a teen, there were 500 or 600cc dirt bikes and "trail" bikes. But I had never been on one and didn't know anything about them.

I had heard that the thought of a 600cc "motocross" bike was ridiculous, because it would be too heavy. From my understanding, the motocross races came in two flavors — 125cc and 250cc. Both of those were obviously a far cry from 600ccs.

Still, I was intrigued.

Before I could act on my curiosity, though, my desire for another big street bike — one that I could understand — got the best of me. Anyone who rides and has owned bikes, and then is without one is well aware of the feeling. If bikes are in your blood, and you are without one, every time you hear the sound, you can't help but look. Actually, you don't want to help it; you are dying to look.

Every time you walk past a bike, you stop to check it out, and every bike you hear reminds you of what you are missing out on.

The modern acronym FOMO stands for Fear of Missing Out. When you've had a bike and now you don't, you don't have FOMO, you have YKTYAMO — You Know That You Are Missing Out. And I had it bad.

Yes, I had my 250, but that was just a bike to play around with the kids on. There was no way that the 250 could relieve my YKTYAMO. And apparently, Sherry couldn't take the sad look on my face any longer.

She decided that what I needed to cheer me up in life was another Harley, and I couldn't disagree.

I had loved the Fatboy so much that another Harley sounded great. This time, though, I would get the few things that I missed out on with the Fatboy.

Yes, the Fatboy was fantastic. And yes, it was one of the best things that I had ever owned. But still, it was missing a couple of things that would have made it perfect.

The Fatboy had virtually no way to carry anything — not without strapping on a bag of some kind, and that would mess up the look. Even multiple types of eye protection or hats for changing weather and conditions would tax the capabilities.

Equally lacking was any way to have a soundtrack for the rides that I would take.

During my time in the Marine Corps, I often thought that what was lacking was background music. We would do some things that were really cool, by any measure, and the weapons made some awesome sounds, but it was always lacking a score.

Now, with my new Harley, that would be fixed. I would get a Street Glide and have plenty of room for storage and the ability to not just have music, but share it with the world — whether they liked it or not.

Sherry did some research and realized that doing what I had done before I met her was not the smartest thing. Spending thousands on extra chrome and accessories just meant that you would lose that much more money when you went to sell the bike later — which experience showed would always happen.

I had lost thousands on the Fatboy, and hoped not to have that happen again.

Harley makes something called a CVO model, I found out. It stands for Custom Vehicle Operation, and it means, allegedly, that the bike is essentially hand-built, rather than coming off the standard assembly line. More importantly, the CVO models come with several nice "extras" built in or on them.

The one we picked out was metallic black with flames "hidden" in the paint in certain spots. And being that it was a CVO, it allegedly would keep its value — or at least more so than models that were not CVOs.

I got the Street Glide, paid way too much for it, and had my next Harley. It was absolutely beautiful. It was the exact look that I was going for. It had everything that I wanted, including an extra dimension to the sound system. It had speakers in the front, speakers in the top of the saddle bags, and even had a lower fairing with speakers, which the Standard Street Glide did not have.

I got exactly what I wanted. And after a few short months, I hated it.

Unlike the Fatboy, this Street Glide was not a part of me. It did not move intuitively and it was not comfortable to ride.

The sound system, the storage system, the reliability — all of that was great. As an off-the-showroom-floor showpiece, it was tops. I didn't have to add anything extra to it — except for maybe some slip-on pipes.

It was a beautiful showpiece — and for me, it was very unenjoyable to ride.

The sensation was different than that of the FJ, but the concept was the same. That is, I never felt like I was in complete control.

With the DT, the Virago, the XR, the CRF, the Sportster and certainly the Fatboy, the bike and I were one. Even the Orange Junkpile, felt more a part of me than the Street Glide ever did.

In some sense it felt like I was sitting on a couch with a motor that was meant for long, straight lines.

Plenty of people love Street Glides. I didn't.

It was heavy — over 800 pounds (maybe closer to 900) without me or gear — and bulky and generally more of an ordeal to take out than something to look forward to.

Even so, I now had it, and I tried to make the best of it and get some rides in.

I took it to see the 1890s UFO Crash Site and Alien Gravesite in Aurora, Texas. We went to Machine Gun Kelly's grave site in Cottondale, Texas. And I took it on a couple of HOG rides.

After a relatively short period of time and with relatively few miles on it, though, I had had enough. I wanted to get back to riding something that I looked forward to, and I had seen something on a group ride that looked interesting. It was a Gunship Grey CVO Road Glide.

To be fair, the day I test drove the Street Glide, I had been encouraged by the salesman to try out the Road Glide also. But, I didn't. I was absolutely convinced that the Street Glide was for me.

One day, though, while window shopping in the local Harley dealership, I started talking with the salesman about the Road Glide, and we went for a test ride.

Ahhhhh....this....THIS was what I needed. And I was hooked.

I traded in the Street Glide and got the Road Glide. It was beautiful — even more beautiful than the Street Glide, I thought, and it was almost perfect.

One of the only things that I thought about changing on the Street Glide had been the handlebars. The handlebars that I ended up with on the Fatboy years earlier were so perfect, that I thought that if I could recreate that, maybe I would enjoy the ride on the new bike more.

The problem with the Street Glide though, when it came to handlebars, was that Ape Hangers just didn't look right on it. That was my opinion, anyway.

Some people had them, and presumably liked them, but given that the Street Glide had turned out to be more of a showpiece than a desired ride, the last thing I wanted to do was mess up the look. And besides, given the experience with the Fatboy of guessing wrong on the first set of Apes, what if I did that? The Street Glide was expensive enough, without throwing good money after bad.

The Road Glide, though, was a whole different ball game. This bike was so perfect — I thought — that if I could make it even perfecter, it would be like dying and going to heaven.

The salesman, Freddy a/k/a Speedy, was great to work with and helped me pick the perfect Apes. Those plus the Slip-ons made everything look incredible, and surely I would enjoy every ride.

As an aside, even a great ride on any of these newer Harleys couldn't be as good as the rides "back in the day," I found out. At some point after my Fatboy days and before I got the Street Glide, the government decided that it would pass a rule that prevents newer Harleys from sounding as cool as they did throughout all of their prior history.

Allegedly, if you know what you are doing, you can get the sound back, but then that somehow allegedly voids your warranty.

Nevertheless, even if the Road Glide could not sound as awesome as the Fatboy, I anticipated that the rides would be just as good.

Like the Street Glide, the Road Glide was very heavy, but the fact that the front fairing was not attached to the handlebars made riding, especially at slower speeds, easier. I was looking forward to hopefully, finally, taking those long adventure trips that I had always dreamed of.

***

The long trips never materialized, though. I took a few day trips around North Texas and even took an overnighter up to Oklahoma to visit a motorcycle museum, but it turned out to be closed, so even that was not the stuff of dreams.

As with the Street Glide, I could never get that comfortable feeling that I had with my earlier bikes.

The Street Glide and Road Glide are both built on a touring frame, and the Fatboy was built on the Softail frame. The difference, at least to me, was beyond noticeable. It was everything — at least when it came to comfort and confidence in riding.

As with the Street Glide, the Road Glide was a true showpiece. It was a bike that anyone would be proud to own. The richness of the color, the custom wheels, and the styling were all magnificent. And though it would be a stretch to say that I hated riding it — the way I did the Street Glide — I did not enjoy it very much. I couldn't relax on it, even to the extent a rider should be able to on the street.

It seemed like my days with the Road Glide were numbered. But that was okay, because I was starting to explore another path.

CHAPTER TEN

ADVENTURE BIKES – THE PLAN

When Zach turned about 10 or 11, he had outgrown the CRF 50, and he seemed to have riding in his blood to some extent. It was time to get him a bigger bike.

He wouldn't be able to fit on the 250 for several more years, so something in between needed to be found. He loved green, and had fallen in love with the look of Kawasakis. Although I remembered not liking them much in my youth, Top Gun and the years since seemed to have buoyed their standing in the motorcycle world. Also, I didn't want to rain on Zach's parade.

So, into the Kawasaki dealership we went.

The KLX 110s seemed to be a good fit for him, and there was even one that my wife expressed an interest in learning on. That was all great.

The thing that had me tantalized, though, was this large on-off that I saw sitting there.

I had heard about the KLR 650, because I had started exploring the world of Adventure Bikes. These, from what I could tell, were not bikes upon which one could simply have an adventure. In my mind, any bike could provide that. This was a "new" genre that the motorcycling world was calling Adventure Biking.

In reality, at least to me, these were on-off...Enduro...Trail bikes — along the same lines as the ones that I and all of my friends had as teens. But it was as though the world had forgotten them and now someone was trying to brand them anew — trying to make the riding world think that something new had been invented.

As it was explained to me at the Kawasaki dealership, the KLR was on the way out. The year we were there was going to be the last year of them, although from what I was told, they had been reliable workhorses for years.

I don't remember where I first heard of the KLR, and I don't remember the exact chronology of my introduction to the Adventure world, but somewhere along the lines, I listened to *Jupiter's Travels* on audiobook. Additionally, I found *Adventure Rider Radio* on podcast, along with its companion show, *ARR RAW*. Those and more piqued my interest.

I had been an admirer of Road Runner magazine for a while and found Ride Texas magazine too. They both seemed to feature more and more of the Adventure Bikes, or at least show them in more photos than I had seen in the past.

I began searching and trying to understand what the whole Adventure Bike "thing" was, and found Adventure Rider Magazine.

Despite my research, though, I couldn't tell to what extent this "new" world was real, and to what extent it was just a marketing scheme.

I had seen some marketing hyperbole in my work life — who hasn't? In the legal world, several years earlier, there was this "new" thing introduced. It was "a whole new way" to handle your dispute. "You don't need courts!"

Ha! They just weren't telling the whole story.

The imprecise truths were promulgated by some lawyers who figured that with some slight word play, they could make the world think that they had found the Holy Grail of dispute resolution. They hadn't. It didn't exist — at least not like they wanted the public to think.

Everyone has heard more than they want to hear in life of this product and that and how they are supposedly better than before. They have a "New Formula!" or are "New and Improved!"

Was that what I had found? Was this a marketing ploy of some sort or a whole new realm that would lead to places I had never been, figuratively and literally?

***

I didn't need another bike in the conventional sense — but in the Biker sense, I needed another bike. I already had the Harley and the CRF, and I needed more.

Once, when I asked my wife how many horses she wanted, she responded, "All of them." I felt the same way about bikes.

I wish I had kept my DT. I wish I could have kept my Virago. I even wish I had kept the FJ. And on and on.

I didn't want to make that mistake again. Just because I had a bike — or two — didn't mean that I didn't need another one. This one was different. And maybe, just maybe, this new bike would lead me to the World that I had dreamed of finding as a kid, the World that I envisioned while staring at brochures and other people's bikes and wishing I could do all of the magical things that I could dream up and that the photos showed.

The KLR on the showroom floor was beautiful, in its own way. It had sharper lines than the street bikes that I had owned, and was "boxier." I assumed that all of that was utilitarian, but didn't care if it wasn't. If I was going to enter this new world, I didn't want to enter by trying to buy the biggest and best State-of-the-Art "superbike." I was more than okay just dipping my toe in the water at first.

One of the coolest things, I thought, about the KLR, and something that would immediately make me part of the Adventure Bike crowd, was the "crash bars." I don't even remember the actual name that either the salesperson or Kawasaki had for them, but wrapped around the bike was steel tubing that would protect the bike in the event of a fall, crash, etc.

Sherry was agreeable — she didn't intend to ever get on it anyway — and we made the deal for the two KLXs and the KLR. Three new bikes in one day — that beat the old record of two.

Now, I had a bike that would legitimately allow me to explore the Adventure world.

Looking back on it, I think that I had even set out a time or two on the CRF, hoping to find the secret portal to that new World, but I felt more like a fraud than anything else. I had packed a couple of things onto the CRF, bungee'd them on, and set out for the day. It gave me a little of the feel of my time as a teenager trying to replicate the brochure photos, but I wanted more, and now I could find it with the KLR, I hoped.

With YouTube and Vimeo, I started finding other details and parts of the New World. I found out that there was a Trans-America Trail (TAT) and that their was a group, thing, or both called BDR — Backcountry Discovery Routes.

I looked for any documentaries that I could find, whether by experts or amateurs, that would help me understand more about my new fascination.

I was particularly interested in the really big bikes. Yes, I had just gotten a KLR, but the 1200 models that BMW and KTM offered looked crazy, and I simply did not understand them.

***

The first thing that seemed to be universally true about Adventure Riding was that it was all about off-road riding. The implication was that, just like I envisioned and to some limited extent experienced with my Orange Trash Heap and DT, the "on" part of the on-off was just a means to get to the "off," without having to deal with law enforcement or having a truck or trailer.

That sounded great!

And what seemed to be really interesting was not just the idea of riding in circles, as I did in my teens and with Zach, but riding straight distances for a long way. The whole point of having the KLR — and maybe later something bigger and bolder — was to go places that my Harley couldn't, at least not with my skill set. Sure, I guess great or even very good riders could probably take my Road Glide around a motocross track, but I didn't even want to take it to places that could allow for any rocks or sticks to get near it.

The KLR could not only go to places that the Harley could only dream of, it was made for it.

I would watch, I would read, I would set out looking for op-portunities. But, living in the Dallas — Fort Worth area did not provide anything much that I could find. I had no idea where to go to find dirt roads that would lead to remote areas, so I would ride to the less developed areas and just explore.

I would find a half-mile road here or a couple mile road there. I would find a dirt road leading somewhere that wasn't marked "no trespassing," and I tried all of those. Is this it? Am I Adventure Biking?

Certainly not like what I saw in some of the videos, heard on the podcasts, and read about, I wasn't. My exploring was fun, but it wasn't scratching the itch. It wasn't satisfying my desire for real adventure. And it was not making me feel like the Adventure Motorcyclist that I wanted to be.

I needed a plan.

***

Years earlier, when I had started my solo law practice with no money and no clients — after leaving a highly paid law firm — I knew that I had to make money fast. I had plenty of debt, a small child, and a stay-at-home wife. I needed a plan then, and I came up with one that worked remarkably well. It was a five-part plan for how to get clients, and how to make money doing things like teaching law classes, while I built up my book of business.

Prior to law school, I had learned planning from the Marine Corps. The Corps specialized in planning and in teaching its Officers how to think through and make plans for everything from a simple frontal assault, to a long-range combat patrol, to a full Amphibious Assault by a Battalion Landing Team against the combined forces of The Threat. I knew how to do all of that and more.

So, this should be simple. I just needed to take myself from where I was in the motorcycling world to where all these Adventure Riders were.

The first phase of my journey was all I was planning for now. It would involve a great deal of education. I needed to learn more about the World, the bikes, the gear, and anything else that I might not know that I didn't know.

Step One would be going to the International Motorcycle Show which came to Dallas every year.

Assuming that I liked what I found out at the Motorcycle Show, Step Two would be renting a big Adventure Bike to just know a little more about it before I went on to Step Three.

Step Three would be going to learn about how to ride the big bike from the experts.

Step Four would be going to a Backcountry Discovery Route event to learn more about it.

And the final step, Step Five, would be putting it all together during one of those training and riding trips that are advertised all over the place in the Adventure Bike World.

The Plan was set. It was time to become an Adventure Rider — at last.

Chapter Eleven

International Motorcycle Show

B ack before the coronavirus ruined so many things in the world, Dallas — and a number of other cities around the U.S. — would host what was labeled an International Motorcycle Show every year. I had heard about it for a long time, but had never been. So, I wasn't exactly sure what it was.

Looking back on it now, it seems odd that I had never gone to the IMS. It was relatively close to me, and I spent considerable time in dealerships during my youth staring at bikes and a great amount of time at Strokers, in my more recent past, doing the same thing. I loved looking at bikes.

I guess, though, that once I started owning bikes of my own I had not always loved all things about all bikes. I think that at times

I suffered from the idea that whatever I had was the best and other types of biking didn't need to be considered.

When I was riding on-off bikes as a youth, they were the only things that really mattered. When I rode the Virago, well, at that point I was probably too busy with either the Marine Corps or Law School to think of much else.

I got interested in the FJ and Sport Touring, and it suddenly mattered, until I found out that it apparently was not for me.

Harleys are, for the most part, their own animal. And anyone who loved them — including me — would often see plenty of them at various dealerships and then at Strokers.

As I got older, I think that I gained an appreciation for all of the different aspects of motorcycling in a way that I never had before. I started to really find everything from Drag Racing bikes to Moto GP to Motocross to Trials to Flat Tracking to be fascinating to a greater degree than I had since my BMX years as a young teenager. And now, a big part of my fascination and curiosity was the Adventure World.

Whatever had caused me to never go before, it was gone now. This was going to be the first step that I would need to begin to find out the answers to my questions. My plan was to learn what I didn't know, and needed to know.

***

Almost immediately upon walking in, I realized how wrong I had been to have never gone to the Show before. If every make was not represented, the vast majority were. There were bikes of every shape and size at the show, and I would be able to compare and contrast the Adventure Models from all of the different players. This was 2019, and by this time, they all seemed to have gotten into the game.

Of course, the two that I was most interested in were BMW and KTM. From everything I had seen and heard and read, these were the top dogs.

As a teen, I had determined that Yamaha was the best bike for the money — at least that I would ever be able to afford — and I was exceptionally happy with all of the Yamahas I had owned. But even then, the things I read led me to the conclusion that the best bike made was BMW.

I knew that German vehicle craftsmanship had an excellent reputation, and the things I read convinced me in my youth that the BMWs made then were the smoothest, most reliable, most technologically advanced machines on the road. And that last part was important — on the road.

I'm not sure that as a teen, or even anytime before my new wonderment with Adventure Bikes, I had ever thought of BMWs as being ridden off-road. Maybe I had seen some pictures, but they certainly were not what came to mind when I thought of off road riding.

When it came to KTM, that was a whole other thing entirely. I knew of KTM, but only in the way that I knew of Bultaco and Husqvarna and other rarely seen bikes. I didn't have a bad impression of them. I didn't have any impression. I had never considered owning one, and growing up I was either taught or just picked up that "off brand" vehicles were harder to get fixed, so be careful before you buy one.

But everything I had seen about KTM, including their ads, made me think that they needed to be seriously considered with BMW.

***

The Bike Show would be my chance to find out if any other bikes needed to be in the conversation. Was it just KTM and BMW, or did I need to consider Honda and the others as well?

Were my thoughts of riding the big bikes just the stuff of fantasy? Did I need to be satisfied just riding my KLR on the occasional dirt road that I could find, and the rest was more in the realm of things that only "other people" did?

The Show was going to be an opportunity to learn much more than just which manufacturer I liked, though. I was very interested in this whole BDR thing, and they were going to have programs and classes at the show. There was gear there, so I could see what all of the ads in the magazines were trying to sell me — and maybe figure out why in the world they would be asking the high prices that they were for so much of the gear.

The best part of The Show, I discovered, was the other vendors — the ones selling the trips. This is what I was interested in.

I was confident that I would make it through Phase One of my journey to the Adventure Bike World — all five steps in the phase

— and I was anxious to begin the planning for Phase Two and beyond. I wanted to get past the training and learning phase and on to the exciting travel phase.

And wow, were there vendors there. There were trips being sold to South America, Africa, Mongolia, Canada, Ireland, and more. Interestingly, what I never heard or read from any of the vendors was, "Keep in mind, your riding skills may not be anywhere close to good enough to make this trip," at least not in those words.

Every one of the Vendors that I spoke with was very nice and very encouraging. They all had great things to say about the trips they were selling, which shouldn't have come as any surprise.

The most memorable vendor that I talked to was Rene Cormier of Renedian Motorcycle Tours. He had tours going to various parts of Africa, Mongolia, and Canada, for sure. He may have had more than that, because I know as of this writing, in addition to those places, he has trips to South America, New Zealand, and Scotland.

Rene was probably the first person that I met in the real Adventure World, and he was a great ambassador for it. I recall thinking, "If everyone in the Adventure World is this friendly and helpful and genuine, I may have found a new home."

I talked to Rene about going on the various trips, and the thing that I noticed and would continue to, as I researched more and more about various trips, was the reference to "experience riding off-road."

The literature would say, "this much of this trip" was off road..."that much of that trip" was on road, and the rest was off. "Off-road riding experience" was suggested for this trip or that.

The off-road experience thing wasn't just with Rene's trips — that semi-prerequisite seemed to be all of them. That is, all of the ones that I was interested in.

Road Runner magazine and other outlets had no shortage of advertised trips that were nothing but pavement. They didn't even mention off-road. And many of the bikes you would be on wouldn't do very well if you accidentally took them off-road.

I knew I could do those trips. I didn't want that kind of riding, any longer. I wanted motorcycling that Tarzan would be proud of. I wanted to explore.

But, none of the "off-road riding" statements deterred my thinking and the beginning of my tentative Phase Two plans — what I would do after I was done with the learning phase. After all, I had been riding off-road since I was a kid.

My neighbor's backyard where I hit the fence was off-road. The field that my friends and I rode in as teens and where I encountered the big pine tree was off-road. Even the Orange Mistake and I had done some off-roading.

Heck, off-road was my middle name. I had been doing that my whole life. This would be no big deal.

* * *

I listened to some of the BDR speakers, but none of what they said made a huge impact. I still couldn't figure them out very well. I looked around at the various makes. None impressed me enough to change my mind from the BMW – KTM dilemma. (Although Honda appeared to be making a big push to really get in the game with their Africa Twin.) And I couldn't find out much about the gear.

I spent most of the time talking about the trips, and probably most of that time at Rene's booth. I bought his book, took his brochures — along with brochures of several other trips from other vendors — and decided after a few hours that I had seen and taken in as much as I could.

True to his character, Rene graciously invited me to ride with him the next morning as he left Dallas, and in retrospect, I really wish I had taken him up on the invitation.

The Show was done, for me.

I had completed Step One. I had at least seen the BMW and KTM up close and asked a few things about them, but didn't feel too far down the road toward my goal. That was okay, though. I knew that this was going to be a process. I couldn't jump into this like I was coming off a high dive; I would have to walk in and try to experience all it had to offer slowly and progressively.

I was confident that Step Three — the BMW Performance Center would answer a lot of my questions about the trip descriptions that referenced off-road riding. I now just needed to get ready for Step Two, finding a real Adventure Bike to rent and ride and begin to try to understand.

Las Vegas, here I come.

Chapter Twelve

Las Vegas –
Gear and All

I looked around on the internet, trying to find a place from which I could rent either a KTM or BMW Adventure Bike. To my surprise, I couldn't find many options. So much for the idea that in the 21st Century everything is available on the Internet. Maybe it was, and I just wasn't good at finding it.

Regardless, I needed to find a rental somewhere. I knew that I did not want to show up for the BMW course having never been on a big Adventure Bike.

It was no longer the size of the engine that caused me the concern I had as a teen — and maybe even in my 20s.

Back then, the same size bike would concern me, if I knew it had more volume in the cylinder(s) than what I felt comfortable with. In hindsight, my fear made little sense, but it was real. I barely knew what a cc was, in relation to a motorcycle engine, but knowing that a bike had too many of them was unnerving.

Now, having been in the world of Harleys, you could tell me that a bike that I was comfortable on had 800ccs or 10,000 — well, maybe not 10,000 — and I didn't really care. I don't even know what my Harleys had, other than the 883, which I assume had somewhere around that number of ccs.

In this new World that I was trying to enter, it was much more about the overall size of the bike. The big KTMs and BMWs looked monstrous. In some ways, they looked bizarrely monstrous. They looked possibly very uncomfortably monstrous.

What was the deal with the gigantic, odd-looking gas tank? Why was it shaped that way? It looked like the whole front end was some sort of Rube Goldberg project.

Everything from the seat to the back looked okay, and the seat height wasn't much of a concern, since at 6'2" I figured I could handle anything mass produced for the general population.

Still, I needed to ride one. I needed to see whether I needed to just stay with the smaller bikes — like the KLR — and leave the monsters for other folks.

Moreover, I needed an extended ride. Not necessarily a trip — in fact probably not, since I wanted to be trained for how to use the big things — but it had to be more than a "test ride."

I had learned the hard way with my Harley experiences that test rides should be renamed "sales rides." I don't know about other people, but for me, there was always some awkwardness of having the salesman as my wingman. I never felt comfortable riding the way I wanted to, and had little control of the route or length of the ride.

Also, when stopped, the salesman was right there. I couldn't just think and feel and get to know the bike, which I wanted to do prior to making any long-term commitment.

And then there was the gear.

Did I need riding gear? Or should I just wear what I wore on my Harley rides? And what's with the prices?

Sherry wanted to get me all of the top-of-the-line riding gear, but that just seemed too expensive. I'm sure it was good, but what if after one trip I decided that it all wasn't for me? I didn't need more things in my closet to gather dust.

My Adventure Rider magazine had full-page ads, every month, for some much more modestly priced gear. They showed jackets and pants from a company called MotoNation and they were much more modestly priced. Would they be as good as everyone said the most expensive gear was? Maybe or maybe not. But for the price, I figured that I could just find out for myself.

***

I found that BMW GS 1200s could be rented. But from what I could find, only a few spots around the country had them.

Finding the GS rentals was a step in the right direction, but I really wanted the Adventure model. I didn't plan to do any adventuring with it, but I knew that I wanted to try a model as close to what I would be thinking of getting as possible — and as similar to what the BMW school would have for the course I would be taking.

I don't think that I ever saw a place that rented the big KTMs, but that was okay. Step Two was about trying the size and shape of these things, and from looking at the Motorcycle Show and dealerships, the big KTM and the big BMW were close enough in overall dimensions that renting either would be okay.

As I recall, the only two rental spots that I could find for the big BMWs were Miami, Florida, and Las Vegas, Nevada. Having grown up in Florida, I had no interest in renting an Adventure Bike anywhere near Miami. The population density alone was more than enough to get that location crossed off the list.

Additionally, though, the other Steps that I had planned involved Western travel, something that was much closer to Las Vegas, once outside the congested areas.

Besides, I loved going to Las Vegas, and one of my best friends would be willing to go there with me, although not for the ride.

***

I packed all of my new gear. I had my Bell MX-9 helmet — again, a bargain choice, but I loved Bell from my youth — my inexpensive, non-top-of-the-line Motocross boots, and my MotoNation Jacket and pants. I also had at least one pair of gloves that would work, sunglasses, etc.

I remember flying out, with my helmet bag in the overhead and feeling like I was embarking on some level of an adventure. This wasn't an Adventure with a capital A — it's not like I was flying to

Mongolia with Rene Courmier and his gang, but it was out of my knowledge base, so a little out of my comfort zone.

The uneasiness really hit the next day, when I was at the hotel, getting dressed and heading downstairs. I felt a great deal like I was getting ready for a costume party. I was going as an Adventure Rider.

***

With the Harley and other bikes, I wore what felt natural and comfortable. With the XR I had owned, I wore some version of a motocross outfit, some type of motocross boot, and maybe a used chest protector over my shirt — or maybe not. I was just riding in fields, after all.

With the CRF and even the KLR, the thought of particular riding gear seemed silly. As long as I had my helmet and gloves and long pants and some kind of half-decent footwear, I felt okay. it was just motorcycling as I had always known it.

Now, though, there seemed to be an expectation from the Adventure Universe of something more. One couldn't enter this World with just whatever they had on. Why not? I don't know.

If the weather allowed it, I would wear a leather jacket when I rode my Harleys, and I knew that doing so provided more protection if, God forbid, I went down. But the weather determined what I wore.

This new World did not allow the weather to dictate what happened within it. To be a part of it — from everything I had seen and read — one had to dress the part. So, I did.

I remember looking at myself in the mirror and feeling like an imposter, but luckily, it did feel a little like a snow skiing outfit, which I had worn many times and was comfortable in — of course I had always done so around thousands of other skiers dressed similarly.

And though I felt strange going down in the fancy Las Vegas Strip elevator dressed in my new outfit, carrying a helmet, and then getting in an Uber, I figured that this was the only way to find the entrance to the New World.

***

I got to the dealership where I had rented the GS 1200. And at that point, was still hoping that it was going to turn out to be a GSA.

This was some European Motorcycle dealership, and apparently they sold several different makes. One of the counters in the back functioned as the Rental Shop for the dealership.

Still feeling a little fraudulent and anxious, I went to where the sign told me to. It was a Thursday morning and about 10:00 a.m. This was clearly not the busy time for the dealer — which was fine with me.

I had rented a zillion cars, some moving trucks, and even some boats and jet skis in my life, but I had never rented a motorcycle. I assumed that it would be about the same, except that I assumed that they might be more worried than the others about me bringing it back in pieces.

The guy at the dealership was nice, though, and helpful. He gave me information about interesting rides that I might take and all the basics for the bike. I tried my best to listen, since this GS was far more technologically advanced than the KLR or CRF, and was nothing at all like my Harleys.

I recall asking a couple of times about locking and unlocking and starting the bike, since it seemed like it would be a particularly bad idea to get out in the desert, switch the bike off to look around, and then not be able to get it restarted. Moreover, I was pretty sure that just about anywhere I rode outside of Las Vegas proper would have limited cell service, and I had no interest in having to "find" my way back to civilization, especially just to call the dealership and ask how to start the bike, and then re-find the bike and come home, feeling even more like a fraud.

***

The bike was nice. It was not brand new, but it was in great shape, and though not a GSA, it was much closer to what I wanted to learn at the BMW Center than anything else I had ever been on.

I checked to make sure that I knew how to open the gas tank to get fuel and cranked the bike up. I'm pretty sure that before I took off, I turned the bike off and on a time or two to be sure I knew how, and then was as ready to go as I was going to be.

The first thing that impressed me was how smooth the bike was. I had had several bikes that I loved, but none this smooth. I cruised some of the local back streets, just to get the feel of the bike, and then set out for some adventure.

I first rode to Red Rock Canyon. It was a good first ride, and the GS was easy to ride. It continued to be unbelievably smooth. I parked the bike a few times and got on and off it enough times that I was feeling more comfortable with it, though it still seemed to be a very odd-shaped bike.

After Red Rock, I decided that I would ride further away from Las Vegas and explore a small town or two. The one thing that I noticed about the bike, while tooling around at low speeds in one of the towns, and just trying to get more comfortable on it, was the torque.

The XR was the only bike that I had ever owned that I could easily pop a wheelie on. In fact, it was probably the only bike that I had ever ridden that could pop one at all. Now, I had found another one that could!

When I started moving and was at creeping speed and gave the GS even a half a wrist full of throttle, the front end would come up.

The first time it happened, I wasn't sure that it really had, so I did it a few more times to be sure. Once I was positive that I could do it if I wanted to, I reminded myself that I wasn't a good enough rider to be experimenting with wheelies on a side street in Nowhere, Nevada, and that I probably wasn't strong enough to pick the bike up, if I dropped it.

Of course there was also the issue of the bike not being mine, and the last thing I needed was a repair bill from the dealership. So, I stopped playing, but not before I was thoroughly impressed with the BMW's power and its smooth as silk ride.

***

I rode some more, continued to experiment with the devices on the bike, and headed back toward Las Vegas. I don't remember where all I rode, but I was happy with all of it.

I tried to find some "off-road" riding that seemed like something that would not cause me to drop the bike, but found very little. I was being particularly cautious, both because it was a rental and it had street tires.

This bike was meant for the road, and with the totality of the circumstances being what they were, I didn't need to push my luck.

I remember riding the bike back to the parking garage at Mandalay Bay Casino at the end of the day, and feeling content that I had gotten the experience that I wanted with the GS.

It hadn't been everything I wanted, but that would come soon enough at the Performance Center. This extended "test ride" was perfect. I could take my time doing what I wanted with no one looking over my shoulder, and I was very happy with the way the bike performed.

The next day, I took the bike back to the dealership, checked it back in, and took an Uber back to Mandalay, feeling less like a fraud than I had the day before.

My trek toward being an Adventure Rider was going well. I had Two Steps down, and both had gone as planned. I was counting on even bigger things and even more success from here on.

Time would tell.

Chapter Thirteen

BMW PERFORMANCE CENTER

I don't even remember how I first heard about it. It is an amazing place where expert instructors can teach you more than you can learn about driving sports cars, SUVs, and motorcycles — both on-road and off.

The idea of going to the Center came as a natural part of my plan to become the kind of Adventure Rider that could take advantage of all of those exotic trips I had seen advertised. They all looked and sounded amazing and though I wanted to go, I didn't want to get in over my head.

I wasn't sure that I needed all of this training — after all, I had been riding off-road for decades, I thought. But maybe I can learn the nuances of riding one of these Monster Bikes off-road. I knew that I didn't know that.

I looked for answers online and looked for any photos or videos that I could find explaining what the Motorrad Off Road Course was and who it was geared for.

First, I needed to figure out what the heck "Motorrad" was — what exactly was "BMW Motorrad"?

I had owned a BMW convertible in my single days, so I was not totally unfamiliar with the brand, but I certainly did not understand all of their nomenclature and labeling.

It turns out that "Motorrad" just means "Motorcycle" in German.

I looked online at the options for the courses that were offered and saw that I could take a one-day or two-day course. I wanted all the education that I could get, since I hoped to be very comfortable on the GSA by the end of the course, and also, I hoped to use the course to help me determine if the GSA was the bike for me.

So the Two-Day Off Road Course it was. The few photos and videos that the Center had online made it look awesome. I don't recall seeing anything death-defying. It just looked like guys who were about my age riding around off-road and learning some "extra" things that I figured I could take or leave — like "burnouts" in the dirt.

In getting my plans together, I determined that I could kill two birds with one stone. I had wanted to spend some time on the Appalachian Trail since my childhood. So, I decided to try to work that into the trip.

One time, when I was probably 8 or 9, my family was close to the Appalachian Trail in North Georgia. We lived in Atlanta at the time.

My dad, having grown up in Atlanta and being fond of camping, was well aware of the Trail.

We stopped at a spot where we could enter the Trail one day, and my dad took my brother and me on a short "hike." I doubt that it was any more than 15 or 20 minutes, but it made a permanent impression. I thought the Trail was cool, and so in my adventure-seeking mind, it was included as a goal.

I had never made it back to the Trail, but given that the southern portion of it is roughly between Atlanta and the Performance Center, this would be my chance. I could fly into Atlanta, rent a car, spend a day hiking the AT, then head on over to Spartanburg, South Carolina, and enjoy the Two-Day Motorrad course.

Perfect.

***

Once I had that plan in mind and pretty much figured out, it was time to improve it. If there was one thing better than hiking and motorcycling, it would be hiking and motorcycling with an old friend. And as it turns out, one of my oldest friends from childhood lived in Atlanta, had a great deal of experience on the AT — as the Trail was called — and knew how to ride motorcycles.

To paraphrase Flounder in *Animal House*, "Oh boy, this is gonna be great!"

I contacted my friend and he was up for it. He tried to talk me out of the AT and onto another trail, but the other one had not been the stuff of my dreams, so I insisted on the AT.

I explained that I did not want to do much. I only wanted to take an easy stroll — maybe an hour out and an hour back. And I wanted to stay on "non-challenging" parts of the Trail.

The focus of this trip was the Performance Center, and I knew enough about the AT to know that it could become challenging. I wanted to save my strength for the Performance Center.

He understood and we agreed.

He, though, had some questions about the Adventure Bike World. Whereas I had been studying it for quite some time at that point, he was new to the idea.

He loved the outdoors and was very experienced in rock climbing, white water kayaking, and hiking, but all of his time on a motorcycle was on the street.

Like me, prior to getting into the Adventure World, he did not have the "necessary" gear. I'm not even sure that at that point he had a helmet, because he had been without a bike for a while.

I talked him through the gear that I had assembled, but was candid about the fact that I was still experimenting and trying to understand it all. As a part of the experimenting, being at the Center would presumably allow us to interact with other riders and maybe we could learn from them and the instructors what was actually needed and what was just costume-wear.

We finished making plans and booking everything, and the itinerary was set. I would fly to Atlanta, get to his place, spend the night, get up the next day and do a nice, easy, short hike on the AT.

Following the easy hike, we would get back to his place in Atlanta in good enough shape to get a good night's sleep and get up the next day to head to Spartanburg. The next day, we would start the BMW Course and have those two days of fun along with the hiking day. All in all, we would have several days of non-stop fun, with a little learning mixed in.

Ha!

***

The next day, we got up, had breakfast at some local place, threw our gear in the car and headed for a spot to enter the AT. I still had memories of being at the place I wanted us to go, but my friend had other plans.

He assured me that he knew best.

We got to a parking lot where hikers could leave their vehicles and easily hop on the AT. We put our light packs on and headed out — or I should say "up."

As I recall, the very first thing we did was start a climb. This was no Mount Everest — not even close. For anyone, even me, this initial climb, and the next couple, would have been no big deal, if we had stuck to the plan.

When I say climb, I simply mean we were headed uphill. There were ups and downs along the way and none of the entire day was too awfully challenging, in and of itself. But, the fact was that we had deviated substantially from the plan.

My friend had — for reasons only he knows — taken us on a much longer and harder trek than I had wanted and we had agreed to. By the time we were done with our AT hike, I was pretty tired, and my legs had used a lot of what they had.

***

The fact is that my legs were never very strong. I was never one of those guys that could put plate after plate on the rack on Leg Day. And now, I had even more working against me, medically.

A few years earlier, I had been hospitalized with something called Hyponatremia — low blood sodium. Frankly, when I was rushed to the hospital in an ambulance and later diagnosed with it, I'm not sure that I knew that my blood was supposed to have sodium in it.

As it turns out, without sodium in our blood, important things like our brain, muscles, and heart don't work. They need the conductivity that the sodium helps provide — at least that's what was explained to me, as I was hooked up to IVs to raise my sodium back up to within normal limits.

And here's an interesting note: If you raise blood sodium too quickly, you will permanently destroy your brain. So, there's that.

Anyway, at least since the hospitalization, my legs were even weaker than they would otherwise be. At the time that my friend and I were going to the BMW Center, I didn't have any reason to believe that I was having any significant problems with my sodium, but tests later would show that I was.

In retrospect, the fact that we used more of my energy than I had planned for or should have by walking for several miles on the AT, just prior to going to the Performance Center was not a good idea, to say the least.

***

As we entered Spartanburg, before finding our hotel, we drove by the Center. It was already closed for the day, but at least we could get an idea of what it looked like, so that we could dream about all the fun we would have.

We got up the next day, ate a little at the hotel, and headed for the BMW Performance Center. This course was not inexpensive, but it was going to be well worth it, when we were done. I didn't want to miss a moment of what we had paid for.

I recall that we got there, and started to mingle with some of the other riders who were in the class. The way the Center is set up, there can be several different classes going on on any one day. There may be an SUV class and a Teen Driver course for automobiles and an off-road motorcycle class, as well as other things happening.

So, all of the people who were in the cafeteria area were not from our class. Somehow, after some more coffee, those of us in the Two-Day Off-Road Course were corralled into the classroom that would be ours for the day.

There were eleven of us in the class — students, that is. In addition to us, there was the Head Instructor for our class, plus a couple of Assistant Instructors.

We laid all of our jackets and helmets and stuff around the classroom and settled in for the fun to begin.

***

I think we went around the class, with all of us introducing ourselves and telling something like where we were from and maybe something about our riding experience.

These were all good guys, from everything I could tell. None of the students made any claim to being any kind of expert with motorcycles. I recall that at least one already owned a GSA, and I thought it was odd that someone who had been riding one for some time would then need to be trained on it.

I would find out why.

***

The class started with classroom instruction.

I have bragged about the Center for years now, and this is one of the things that my bragging focuses on — their classroom instruction. As I was to find out later, not all "Motorcycle Instructors" use the same techniques.

At the BMW Center, before you are given a task to execute, you are provided with detailed, careful instruction about all aspects of it. The Head Instructor talked to us about what the bike would be doing, where our weight needed to be, what to do when this happened or that happened, what not to do, etc., before every "obstacle."

This first part was just the very basics, but it was important. The most important thing that the Instructor made clear was the concept of "Challenge by Choice." I don't know whether that is a trademarked motto of the Performance Center or whether BMW invented it or what, but I thought that it was a fantastic idea, and still do.

The Instructor explained that there was no requirement to do any of the obstacles or "challenges" at the course. Any student could opt out of any of the obstacles, and there would be no coercion, no peer pressure — or instructor pressure.

Better yet, as I found out, the instructors were more than happy to discuss any obstacle in further detail, and help the student determine if the obstacle could be safely encountered and help the student make an informed decision on what to do and what not to do.

As we left the classroom for the first time, I recall being very happy that I was at the school in February. The temperature was perfect for all of the protective gear. I was not going to be too hot or too cold — one less thing to worry about.

We went out to the parking lot behind the building to meet our bikes. And I was extremely impressed with the first thing that the instructor did with the bike.

These were virtually brand new looking GSA 1200s, as I recall. I think the 1250 had just come out or was just about to be released. The only difference between one of these and what could be bought off a showroom floor was that the rear-view mirrors and windshields had been removed, so that we would not have to worry about breaking them if we dropped the bike.

I recall that that was a concern of mine. There is a huge difference between "take this course, and use our bike" and "take this course, and use our bike, and don't worry about anything if the bike gets damaged" — especially in a course that seemed to invite bikes to hit the ground.

We all gathered around the instructor and one of the bikes. We were in a semi-circle, but not too close. The instructor explained that we were not responsible for the bikes and any damage that may be caused to them. He explained that in the course, everyone would fall, and everyone's bike would hit the ground.

He said, "Don't worry about it," or words to that effect, then stepped out of the way and let the beautiful GSA 1200 that he had been holding up fall and hit the pavement. Had that been any bike I had ever owned, I would have been in tears.

But here, the instructor simply said, "See," or something similar, and used the fallen bike as an opportunity to talk to us about what to do if and when our bikes fell, and how to get them picked up.

He explained that when a BMW GSA 1200/1250/etc. starts to fall, we need to get out of the way and let it. This was not my DT 175 that I could easily keep upright, in most situations, simply by putting my foot down. We would be riding in a standing position, and when the bike started to go, we needed to bail out, and let it go.

He pointed out that we needed to hit the kill switch, when we were able to, after a fall, and then proceeded to show us the two techniques for picking up a downed 550-pound bike. Most people, if using the proper technique, can pick up the bike alone. I was not sure that I would be able to.

We got on our bikes and rode out to the spot of our first activity. This wasn't an obstacle, but at least for me, it was a challenge.

In the grand scheme of things, what we did was relatively simple. We just rode the bikes around on flat, sturdy ground to get used to them and then were instructed to start moving around on the bike, as we went. That is, we were supposed to go from sitting to standing and back, and then move both legs to one side of the bike, sit, stand back up and go back to normal standing position with legs on either side, and do the reverse.

I couldn't do it, and in retrospect, this probably should have been a warning sign.

As I mentioned, my legs were not naturally strong, and now, after a day of hiking, they were more exhausted than usual. I soon found out that that was not the only problem.

***

I don't remember where we went from there exactly, but things progressed gradually. We worked on circles and figure 8s and other slow-speed stuff. We practiced higher speed stops in the dirt and getting the bike going and on it from various situations. And we practiced riding through some trees — having to use the slow riding techniques that we had just learned without trees.

I recall that in going through the trees, I saw up close some of the unique dangers of "real" off-road riding.

At some point, somehow, while we were going through the trees, one of my fellow students made some mistake and ended up being pinned to one of the trees by his bike. I can no longer even picture the exact situation, but I recall having to throw my kickstand down quickly and hop off my bike to get to him as fast as possible, as he was yelling for help.

I don't think that he was actually being injured, but he couldn't escape. However this had happened, he had no leverage to get himself out of the situation, and it was definitely an eye opener on the dangers of riding solo in remote places.

I don't remember the exact order of things, but I think we may have made it to lunch that first day with all of us relatively intact. Right before we headed in for lunch, the instructors took us to the track, where the street riding is taught. They let us basically race around the track at high enough speeds that I recall it being one of the most enjoyable parts of the course.

Again, I don't know if I'm remembering the chronology exactly right, but I definitely have vivid memories of the next big eye-opener.

I recall that we had one of our next classes in an outdoor school circle. It made far more sense for these relatively distant challenges to be explained out in the field, without having to return to the schoolroom.

We were out by one of the large hills and close to the smaller ups and downs, which were reminiscent of the whoop de dos that I had known of but never actually ridden. I recall the head instructor explaining to us the importance of throttle control. To emphasize his point, he told us of a student in a past course who got the throttle control wrong.

The Instructor explained that as this former student and his class were working on challenges involving riding up, over the top, and down the largest hill, the student had done something wrong and basically did an Evel Knievel off of the small mountain. The Instructor vividly described how the guy and his bike flew through the air ten or twelve feet off the deck and landed in a very bad way. As I recall, the Instructor said that the student had suffered pretty severe injuries, but survived.

I made a note to self: Don't grab a handful of throttle when going up or near the top of a big hill. These bikes have the power to shoot you off like a bottle rocket.

***

The school circle class ended under the awning outside, near the small ups and downs that we would start with for that type of thing. It was going to involve shifting our weight and gently easing the throttle more and less and more and less and more and less, for as many ups and downs as there were.

It seemed simple. So, we started.

I don't remember why, but not all of the instructors were riding with us. It seems like maybe they showed us how to do it a couple of times, then they decided to take a break, hop off their bikes and just watch and instruct us, as needed, while standing near the small hills and their bikes.

Everything was fine for a while. Everyone seemed to be doing okay. Up and down and up and down. We played follow the leader, and at the end of the row of hills, we circled back and got back at the end of the line. There was no problem.

And then there was.

My friend was going up and down, and was a few bikes ahead of me, when all of a sudden, as he went down, his body weight went to the wrong place and that compelled his right hand to try to stabilize his body — but he wasn't holding onto a fixed object; he was holding onto the throttle.

As he got to the bottom of one down and started up the next up, he accidentally grabbed way too much throttle, which gave the bike way too much juice, and he and his bike shot through the air a couple of feet off the ground and barely missed the instructors' bikes and the instructors, as he landed, and they all dove for cover.

My friend managed to stay on the bike, and somehow get it stopped, and no one was injured, except him. He suffered either a badly sprained or broken ankle, and became casualty number one for our class.

My friend tried to carry on, but it was no use. He was out, and now we were down to ten.

We spent the rest of the day learning about deep sand, and deep gravel, and all kinds of obstacles that were challenging. I don't know whether all but my friend made it to the end of the day, but I think so.

I recall being disappointed earlier in the day, when the instructor indicated that we may stop at 3:00 or 3:30, depending on what people wanted to do, instead of 4:00 or 4:30, which is what the class was scheduled for. But by the end of that first day, I felt like I had taken a beating. The soreness hadn't set in yet, but I had fallen countless times, in every conceivable way, it seemed, and whatever time we called it quits was fine with me.

I'm not 100% certain that ten of us showed up for Day Two, but I know my friend headed back to Atlanta, so I was at the course with whoever else came back for the follow-up day of fun. It seems that early on Day Two, students started dropping like flies.

One may have called it quits after our first break. Seems like two or three said they were done at lunch. And one or more decided they had had enough by the time we got to the early afternoon break.

One way or the other, we were down to three of us by the last couple of hours. The only reason that I was one of the last three was because I was determined to at least be exposed to everything, even if I couldn't do it. I wanted to see all of the obstacles and hear the instructors detail how they should be approached and handled.

My legs were toast, and I was pretty much just an observer on a bike for everything after lunch.

***

After the last break, we were headed for the finish line — figuratively speaking. I recall one of the students who left at the last break saying something to the effect of, "I'm not injured yet, and I want to go ahead and stop before I get hurt."

That didn't mean that the student hadn't fallen. We had all fallen. In fact, I'm pretty sure that we had all fallen more times than we could count — I know I had.

That would soon become relevant.

As we headed for the home stretch, I recall that one or more of the "extra" instructors was off doing other things. There were only three of us left in class, so it seemed like overkill to have more than two instructors.

The Head Instructor was leading the way, and for some reason, the Assistant Instructor was not playing Tail End Charlie — I was.

We were riding through a section of the school's property that we had been to several times. It was not one of my favorites, but it was basically just a path to get us to whatever obstacle we had agreed to end on.

The Head Instructor had given us a choice on how much more to do, and at whatever time in the late afternoon it was, we decided to go do one more thing and then call it. There were only about 20 minutes left in the entire Two-Day experience.

I had loved the course; I had loved the bike; and I had been happy with everything about the entire two day operation, except losing my friend to injury.

We were just motoring along, at a very slow speed, and winding our way along the path through the brush when I came upon a mud puddle. I had gone through these many times over the last 24+ hours, and there was no reason to be concerned.

Then boom!

However I hit it wasn't right. More importantly, my exhaustion had caused me to not have the correct body position — the one I had been taught just the day before. I was sitting down when I should have been standing.

Boom! I was down. Just as I had been many times, but this time something was different.

As the bike went out from under me and my body shot forward, I hit something. I will never know for sure what, but I assume I somehow smashed into the handlebars — I don't think there was anything else to hit.

As I lay on the ground, the rest of the class kept going. They couldn't have known that I was down.

Immediately, I knew something was different. On all of the other wrecks in class, I had hopped right up — even the one (or more) where I partially landed on my head. I had nothing but bruises from the other falls, but this time the pain was very bad, and getting worse.

I think I managed to reach over and kill my bike, and I'm pretty sure that I either hit the weak-sounding horn or at least tried to.

Regardless, after doing what I could, I just lay back and waited for help. I couldn't get up. Maybe if my life depended on it I could have, but it didn't, and I couldn't.

After a couple of minutes, the Assistant Instructor came riding back and found me. I don't recall ever seeing the other students again, but at some point pretty shortly thereafter, the Head Instructor rode up.

As with all motorcycle accidents, the instructors were careful about moving me or removing my helmet, once I convinced them that something was different about this fall. I recall having to make clear that yes, I needed an ambulance.

They called for the emergency help, and then it was a matter of lying there and waiting.

***

The ambulance got there, and by then, the pain was increasing significantly. The crew from the ambulance could not have been nicer, and they got me loaded up.

I have never doubted that I need to be in an ambulance when I have gotten in one, because I can't imagine not caring about them jabbing the things into me like they do, unless that sounded like an improvement.

They took me to one of the local hospitals, and I don't recall which one. From there, things turned miserable.

I have been in ERs more times than I can count, going back to age two. I have been hospitalized a number of times. I have been treated as badly as I was treated at that hospital only one other time. The staff's indifference was difficult to understand, to the point that they put me in a room with no way to communicate with them, closed the door, and went out into some common area and just started having a social hour.

I could see them laughing and talking and having a great day, as I lay there unable to move more than a little bit, unable to get up, and unable to get their attention for the assistance that I needed. I finally used my cell phone to call the hospital's main number and convince the operator that I was, in fact, a patient lying in the ER who needed help.

The staff got word from the operator, or someone, calling them and they finally came back in the room. Several tests were run, and they determined that I had a broken rib and a punctured lung.

In retrospect, even with that diagnosis, it does not seem like my overall pain over the next few days should have been as bad as it was. My non-medical opinion is that all of the other falls were starting to take their toll, along with this significant blunt force trauma.

The care was so horrendous, both in the ER and in the room, that all I wanted to do was get out of there, but I had no realistic way to do it. The doctors told me that if I tried to fly home, I could die, due to the punctured lung. They said that I had to stay in the hospital, and I knew that even if I managed to get out of the hospital and an Uber to my hotel, I would have no realistic way to help myself.

Luckily, I had my cell phone, but the battery was dying, and I did not have the charger, and everyone I could find to ask at the

hospital claimed that no one there had an Apple phone charger —
in the entire hospital staff.

The next morning, a doctor came in and told me that I did not
need the extra procedure that the staff had told me I might need
the day before. He said they were going to release me that day. I
questioned him, since that was completely contrary to what I had
been told the day before — that I would die if I left the hospital.

Whether through miscommunication, neglect, or something
worse, the staff's behavior left me questioning their competence
and honesty.

Either way, I left the hospital the afternoon after the fall, and
took an Uber to my hotel. My wife was on the way to get me. She
had flown from DFW to South Carolina, rented a vehicle, and met
me at the hotel to take me home.

The BMW Performance Center experience was over — for that
time. And I had learned a great many lessons.

Now the question was, would I be healed in time for the next
step of my journey, one of two more that I had already booked and
paid for?

Chapter Fourteen

BACKCOUNTRY DISCOVERY

I watched everything I could find on the BDR — the organization, the routes, the people. They had videos that I purchased through Vimeo and watched and studied. This looked like exactly what I was wanting. That is to say, what I thought I wanted before my Performance Center experience.

Now, having realized that all the slips and falls were not nearly as enjoyable in real life as they look on the BDR videos, I was not so sure what I wanted. "But," I thought, "I know what my problem is...I'm just not ready for the big GSA yet...I'll be fine on the smaller KLR."

I got home from South Carolina and started to recuperate. It was almost exactly two months until the BDR Fundraiser in Borrego Springs, California. I should be healed up and good to go by then.

Even though I had lived in the same county when I was in the Marine Corps at Camp Pendleton — San Diego County — I had never heard of Borrego Springs. It sounded adventurous, though, and I was looking forward to going. I had been hurt on bikes — including both bicycles and motorcycles and other vehicles — plenty of times. An injury wasn't going to stop me.

I knew that the Fundraiser wasn't a "course" like both the Performance Center and the Immersion Trip were, but I still planned to use it as a learning opportunity. My goal was to get there and meet people and play 20 Questions with all of them that I met. I wanted to understand the whole concept, and at this point, with three parts of the plan complete, I still felt like a complete beginner in the Adventure World.

The documentaries, blogs, etc. all talked about getting the GPS Tracks to ride off-road and not get lost. It sounded like doing so was mandatory, at least if you wanted to have a chance of doing a real off-road route safely — in the sense that you would end up where you wanted to end up. Unfortunately, I had no idea how to "get" GPS Tracks. I didn't yet have any type of Garmin and wasn't sure if my cell phone was an option or how it all worked.

I hoped that at Borrego Springs I could find someone who would show me how to do it and let me get in on all the "fun."

***

My plan was to load my KLR into my trailer and drive my F-350 Diesel with the trailer in tow out to Borrego Springs. The BDR had blocked out the entirety of what looked to be a pretty awesome desert hotel with an accompanying RV park.

I figured that I could pull the bike, and stop along the way to ride various parts of the BDR routes of New Mexico and Nevada. I don't recall whether California was not done yet, but for some reason, it was apparently not an option, and I recall being disappointed that the BDR Fundraiser did not involve actually riding on one of the BDR routes.

It seemed like a good plan, but there was one major issue at the outset. I didn't own a motorcycle trailer. So, in addition to healing and getting my bike ready and truck ready, I needed to determine what kind of motorcycle trailer I needed to make this and what I hoped would be many more journeys like this.

I also needed to remember how to tie down a bike properly. Especially one this heavy and for this long a trip.

The KLR was 100 pounds or so lighter than the GSA, and I figured that would solve whatever problem I had riding the GSA and more precisely thought that it would solve the problem that had landed me in the hospital.

I found some great gear online to get my bike set up and had mounted Tusk hard paniers on the KLR — actually, it was more like my 12-year-old son did and I helped[1] — so I figured that I could look like an Adventure Rider, even if I wasn't really one yet.

---

1. See previous note on my relationship with tools.

At pretty much the last minute, things came together and my wife found the perfect trailer for me that was big enough for two or three bikes, depending on the size, had a large ramp, multiple doors, and a double axle. It was perfect, and between it and the relatively new F-350, I had a first-class setup. The fact that the newish truck and new trailer had within them what some would consider an "outdated" KLR was still okay, I figured, because it seemed that everyone loved KLRs — they weren't outdated, they were nostalgic.

The excitement for the trip built and the pain from my South Carolina injury was gone. April got here and it was time to load up and go "join the club."

***

Somewhere early on, I realized that my route wouldn't take me anywhere near enough for me to ride on any of the New Mexico BDR, which was disappointing. That was okay, though; I still had the Nevada BDR between me and Borrego Springs.

I don't recall exactly where I stayed that allowed me to get on the Nevada route, but I recall it being just like in the "official video." Part of the route that I rode was paved, but part was dirt or gravel. And fortunately, this was light gravel, not like the ridiculously deep stuff we trained on at the Performance Center.

I had a SPOT tracking device, so even though I was on my own in an area that was relatively remote, I assumed I was okay. I had all my safety gear on, and my paniers and I felt a little — very little — like an Adventure Rider.

Was this it? Was I doing it?

I wasn't sure.

I rode as much of the BDR as I calculated that I had time for, and certainly did not want to get to any parts that would cause me to have another accident, out on my own. I saw the signs that warned of rattlesnakes, and saw a big snake crossing the road in front of me. I got close enough for a photo, but not close enough to confirm that it was indeed a rattler. Nevertheless, I assumed it was, and chalked that up as part of my adventure building.

I finished with Nevada, loaded back up and headed for Borrego Springs. This was gonna be great!

***

I got to the place that the BDR had rented. I had called ahead to make sure that I understood how the parking would work, and had rented one of the hotel rooms. I wasn't sure what to expect, but I hoped for and fully anticipated the best.

The RV parking was used for people like me who had trucks and trailers to park, as well as for people actually RV'ing it. I had a spot, I over-secured my gear, and went to meet people.

For me, it was like the first time I went to a professional sports event as a teenager. Seeing people in real life that I had seen on screen was surreal. I'm not exactly sure why I felt that way at this event, though, since by this point in life I had met many actual famous people, and had even spoken to a couple of Presidents. For some reason though, I was in awe of the BDR crowd.

Early in my time at the resort, I stumbled upon one of the nicest people that I have ever met in the Adventure World.

I was walking from somewhere to somewhere in the resort, and there were a couple people taking a big bike down out of a pickup truck. I looked, and it was Jocelyn Snow — what I understood to be literally the best female GSA rider in the world. And here she was, all four foot whatever of her. She was tiny.[2]

More importantly, she couldn't have been nicer.

This was someone who — particularly in that world — could have had a real superiority complex, and had a right to one. But she didn't. Not in the least. She was one of the friendliest, most welcoming, and kindest people I met during the entire BDR event. And as it turned out, meeting her would turn out to be a blessing and also what led me to needing a blessing.

As I recall, that first night was some sort of a relatively informal time. we had a meal, after which there was just down time for mingling and meeting various people. Some of the folks were BDR "Staff" — apparently some paid and some volunteer — and some were to at least some extent like me. That is, they were non "BDR Workers" and were, instead, attendees at the Fundraiser to help BDR raise funds.

---

2. Note that "four foot whatever" is just an approximation. I'm sure that she is over five feet tall — at least with boots on.

My memories of how it all evolved are not complete, but I remember thinking, as I met people, that some of them were very friendly and welcoming, and some were less so. I remember finding the mix a bit odd. Nevertheless, it was what it was. And fortunately, those that were friendly far outweighed the others, both in number and my appreciation for them, and as long as I could find out the information that I wanted, like how to download the tracks so that I could have my own adventures, everything would be great.

***

That first night, various groups sat around in the meeting/dining area. There was no organized ride; as such, it was just up to everyone to find people they wanted to ride with — either based on plans made prior to getting there, or while there.

I didn't know anyone, other than those I had met in the few hours I had been there, so I appeared to be somewhat unique. It seemed that everyone else either came to the event with one or more friends or knew others from the past.

Luckily — or so it seemed at the time — I had made friends with several people already. One of those was Jocelyn, and she had introduced me to several others, including what I understood to be the male equivalent of her. That is, the best male GSA rider in the world.

Jocelyn and her friends planned to ride somewhere and do something the next day, leaving at some point shortly after breakfast. She and others invited me to join their group. Although I couldn't tell whether that was agreeable to all in her group, I wasn't going to let that stop me, since I wanted to ride with someone who knew what they were doing, and I knew that she and at least some of her other friends were world-class experts.

In retrospect, that was a mistake.

Everyone in the group had a GSA. I had a KLR. They all could and did go very fast. I couldn't, so didn't.

When we met up and left the next morning, I'm pretty sure that there was less detail given than on any group ride I had ever been on — whether formal or informal. I just recall sort of rolling into line and going.

God was watching over me, however, before we left.

As I was getting my KLR out of the trailer and firing it up, a friendly man walked by who I found out was the owner of Wolfman Motorcycle Luggage. We talked a little and he found out that I was about to leave with the group that included Jocelyn. And he saw my Tusk hard panniers on my bike.

Though I now realize how stupid it was for a rider of my level to have these panniers on the bike for the ride we were about to do, I didn't know it then. The idea of having them on was going to give me that chance to see what it was like to be like the riders in all the videos.

I had watched, and studied, as best I could, the various types of panniers and the pros and cons of each. I wanted to get to the point of being the rider in the videos, and so far — in Las Vegas and South Carolina — all of the riding was done without the Adventure Accessories — at least the ones for the bike.

Yes, I guess the bike I rented in Las Vegas had hard panniers, but I had not been able to ride off road, and it wasn't a GSA — it was just a GS. It didn't count.

I wanted to manufacture the adventure, and loading myself up with all the gear, both on me and the bike, seemed the way to do it.

The Wolfman owner knew better. With a very serious tone, he told me that I needed to take those hard panniers off the bike before I went on the ride I was about to go on. I cannot recall for sure whether he said, "If you don't, you'll regret it," but that was definitely the sense I got.

I owe him a huge debt of gratitude, because he knew what he was talking about and I am certain, looking back, that he saved me from substantial additional injury, severe pain, and possible permanent disability.

***

We left the area, and the group took off like they were shot out of a cannon. They were flying at GSA speeds and I was doing my best at KLR speed to catch up.

The leader pulled over every once in a while to either check the route, allow everyone to catch up, or both.

I stayed with the group, but only because of the generosity of the group. They could have easily left me in the dust at any point.

To my knowledge, we weren't headed anywhere for any event — this wasn't a HOG Group Lunch Ride. We were just riding to ride and go somewhere that either some of those in charge had been to or wanted to explore.

At some point, we turned off of "normal" roads and onto what I understood to be Forest Service Fire Roads. Sometimes we were on dirt roads, and sometimes they were narrow black-topped roads.

I have no idea why I had thought it was a good idea to go somewhere that I had no idea about with a group that were all clearly much better riders than me but I had. And possibly more importantly, all of these superior riders had superior bikes. It was not just the speed on the road. The GSAs were superior in every way. The one "advantage" that the KLR had — lighter weight — was more than made up for by every other technical, mechanical, and ergonomic advantage.

I was in way over my head.

I vividly remember thinking, while negotiating as best I could the hazards of one of the roads as we made our way up some small mountain, that the thing they did not mention at the Performance Center — probably assuming that anyone with a brain would know this — is that all of the individual "challenges" of Adventure Riding do not present themselves in the real world the way they are presented at the Performance Center.

At the Center, it was "now we're doing ruts," and we did ruts, and then, "now we're doing sand," and we did sand, and then, "now we're doing tight turns," etc. Here, multiple challenges came all at once. It was like a video game with no pain-free reset button.

"Off to the left, we have a steep uphill with big rocks and cactus...to your right, you will see a steep downhill that one might even call a cliff to some extent...and in front, you have varying terrain, sometimes loose, sometimes surface sand on asphalt, sometimes rutted, and sometimes with some water or other obstacle..."

To really heighten the experience, there was whatever the wind was doing and the possibilities of animals, birds, etc.

In short, the obstacles were coming in multiples. I was not a good enough rider for all of that — and especially on the KLR.

***

At some point, we were at a stop and Jocelyn or one of the others asked me about standing. I had been negotiating everything while sitting on the KLR.

From the Performance Center, I had at least a basic understanding of the preference/need to stand when off-road and or dealing with various obstacles, but I did not have the ability on the KLR.

At 6'2" and with Motocross boots on, either my dimensions, my skill level, or both simply did not allow me to ride from a standing position on that bike, like we had been taught in South Carolina on the GSAs.

Sadly, I explained that I couldn't, though I understood the suggestion.

I think it was at that same stop that one of the very experienced riders in our group was having a problem with his bike. It was something minor, and simply needed a tie of some type or duct tape or something to fix the issue. But, no one in the group had brought anything like that with them for the ride — except me.

Even though I had followed the advice of the Wolfman owner, I still wanted to feel like an adventurer. To me, that meant making myself and my bike into a rolling Swiss Army knife — ready for anything.

Before I removed the hard panniers, they were loaded with all kinds of things. I may not have been able to deal with any eventuality, but I could have dealt with a lot. Once they were off, I couldn't carry as much, so I couldn't be ready for as much, but I was determined to bring what I could, to get all the Adventure feeling that I could.

I had ties and tape and who knows what else with me. And when it was needed, there I was — very proud to be part of the solution. That was the high point of the ride for me — getting to help. Shortly after though came the low point.

We left the stop and headed out again. As before, I had no real idea where we were going, but we were still on "top" of some small mountain. We were still in the middle of nowhere.

I don't remember exactly what the terrain was, but it was loose. It was some deep sand, with a tighter part of the trail as I recall, and I had to make some maneuver with my bike, right as my bike wanted to do something else.

I had "dabbed" with either foot a few times at this point, and so far, I had made it. This time, I put my left foot down to keep the bike upright, and the bike didn't do what I needed and I was down. Worse, my ankle was twisted under the bike. Crack!

Plenty of people have suffered far worse injuries than me, and I had suffered plenty of problems in the past. Regardless, though, the comparisons don't help when the situation arises again. This was not good.

I had done something to my ankle and it hurt badly. Luckily, I was not the tail of the entire group, and one way or the other, I think the entire group stopped, at least eventually.

Several who were riding with us were extremely kind. I wish I knew all of their names to thank them. They helped get my bike off of me, and get my bike up, and get me up. I could hobble around, but could not walk properly, and clearly had something substantial going on with my ankle. Thankfully, other than that, I was okay — just embarrassed, frustrated, and concerned.

The first part of the analysis was: Could I continue with the ride? Clearly not. I was having enough trouble keeping up when I was 100%; there was no way I even wanted to try to keep up now.

Next was: Could I ride? I didn't think so, at least not with shifting. Given the way my ankle felt, I didn't see how I could operate the shift lever for anything other than getting it from Neutral to 1st.

Jocelyn said that she would take me down on the back of her bike. She would get me out of the off-road, back to the paved roads, and all the way back to the Hotel, if needed. She was an angel. And if there's one thing better than an angel, it's a highly skilled angel.

Although several others were very thoughtful, and may have been willing to do the same thing, if asked. Jocelyn was the only one there that I would have trusted to do it. She was an expert's expert. I knew it, she knew it, and everyone there knew it.

While I trusted Jocelyn, and greatly appreciated the offer, it wouldn't completely solve my problems. I still had the issue of my bike being up on top of this little mountain in California. More importantly, it would be there while I was miles away and unable to get up to it.

We were so far into the backcountry, that it wasn't like I could just drive my truck and trailer from the Hotel to the location and load it up later. If I took Jocelyn up on her offer, I would still have to figure out how to get my bike back.

My memory is that some of the others offered to come up the next day and get it, which I appreciated, but that was going to be a lot of moving parts. I was hurting. I wanted the situation solved, but I wanted to find the simplest way to get from where I was to solved, and be done with the entire situation.

One of the gentlemen there stepped up and was similar to Jocelyn. He offered to give up the rest of his ride to help me.

Either he or one of the others suggested that it may be possible for me to shift, using the back of my boot. I had never thought of that, or heard of it before, but it made perfect sense. I wasn't sure if it would work, but it made sense.

I could use my heel to push down into 1st, and from there, use the back of my heel — carefully — to get the lever up into everything needed from there. If I could make it to some hard pack, the plan made sense, and it seemed the best alternative.

***

We were about 25 miles from the Hotel when I went down, and I'm not sure if that distance was once we got back to the pavement or from the exact spot. Either way, the ride back was not going to be a 10-minute jaunt.

I would need to be careful and deliberate and follow the rider helping me out of the off-road, back to the pavement, and back to the Hotel. So, that's what I did.

We made it back, and the man graciously offered to get me some ice for my ankle, as I made it to my room, where I could really let the frustration of the overall situation sink in.

I was back to my room, back to my stuff, and all in all, things could have been much worse. Given the way I went down, I have no doubt that if God had not put the Wolfman owner in my path that morning, or if he had not been kind enough to offer his advice, or if I had not listened, I would be dealing with something much worse. It seemed that a compound fracture could have easily happened.

As it turned out, I had what I thought was a badly sprained ankle. I needed to ice it down and get some rest and figure out where to go from there, conceptually.

My thoughts quickly turned to the Final Step of my Five-Part Plan — the Immersion Course. I looked at the calendar and confirmed that it was in approximately two months. I had already booked it and paid for it — or at least was committed to.

I looked online to see when the last day to cancel was — it was that day. I had to make an instantaneous decision of whether I was in or out. And I had to make the decision without knowing for sure what was up with my ankle.

I decided that I was in.

***

I had always heard that a person cannot walk on a broken leg or ankle or foot or whatever. The theory was that if the bone that needs to be used is broken, the limb is inoperable.

I could walk — hobble — therefore, my ankle was not broken, I decided. That meant that I should be fine to do the Immersion Course.

I was exhausted and irritated, but I did not want to make a bad decision by making a rash decision. I figured that if the Course was something I had wanted to do when I felt good, it should still be something that I should do.

Besides, if I canceled it, there would not be another one for a while. Even if I didn't "want" to do it or feel like doing it, at that moment, I needed to in order to finish my 5 Step Plan to become an Adventure Rider.

And that was what I needed to do in order to progress to making the exciting trips and doing all of that outrageously fun stuff that the videos and brochures showed me was possible.

The next few hours were kind of a blur. I don't remember the exact chronology, but I do remember that many of the people at the event were very kind. There were people who offered to bring me ice and talked to me about the situation. They offered kind words and words of encouragement and showed genuine concern. Others not so much.

I recall having to hobble to a meal and then listening to some program about upcoming BDR events. But I also recall finding out that an old Marine Corps friend lived in the area and leaving the event to meet him and talk about old times.

Somewhere in all of that, I decided that night that I would load up and leave the next morning, a day early.

I managed to get my bike loaded and gear packed up and loaded in the truck and got up early the next morning. Before virtually anyone was up, I pulled out. I had calculated that I could make it back in two days, if I drove hard enough.

Given the injury, it wasn't like I was going to be stopping to ride, as I had originally planned. And I couldn't even stop and do any sightseeing. But, since it was thankfully my left ankle rather than my right, I could drive.

I pulled out of the area, made it back to the main freeway, and headed East. I was going to get as many miles under my belt as I could before I stopped for the night.

Having driven that general path many times at that point in life, I knew that there were relatively few decent hotels between where I was and where I was going. Yes, I could always think of just going "a little further," at any point in the drive, but the reality was that I had to take the anticipated drive in "chunks."

Once I committed to leaving any city or town along the way, I would need to go another 100 miles or so, before I would get to the next place big enough to have a hotel that I was familiar with.

It wasn't like I could decide at any moment to just drive another 30 minutes like I could along the East Coast or West Coast — from one town of any size to another was a matter of hours, not minutes.

***

I made it out of Borrego Springs and to the Southern California desert in no time. From there, I drove for some time and then got to Arizona. To make it in two days instead of three, I would need to get through all of Arizona and well into New Mexico.

The GPS said that from Borrego Springs to Albuquerque, New Mexico, would be a little more than eleven hours of driving. If I stopped there, I would still have a pretty good drive the next day, and from experience, I knew that there were a couple of towns between there and Texas in which I could stay.

I will never forget getting to the outskirts of Albuquerque as night was falling. The drive had gone reasonably well up to that point, and I still felt pretty good, all things considered. I wanted to keep going. I wanted to make it to at least Santa Rosa, and if possible, Tucumcari, before I stopped.

My ankle was feeling okay, but I wanted to get it propped up and on ice. But what I really wanted was to do that at home. Overall, the BDR event had been a pretty big disappointment for me, and I wanted to be done with this trip.

As night gently fell and my wheels continued to turn, all was pretty good. It even struck me that the light snow that was starting to fall was beautiful, as the lights from my vehicle and others, along with the lessening street lights, hit the flakes.

Albuquerque is no small town, so getting through it, even on the freeway took a few minutes, though I don't remember how long.

I must have been on a mental autopilot and just living the dream, as I continued on the freeway, under the last overpass, and headed out of the city. That is the only way that I can understand why I did not wrap my mind around the danger that I was driving into.

My home was in DFW. It had been for about 30 years. And that's what I was headed back to.

But I had driven cross-country more times than I could remember at that point. Maybe it wasn't as many as it seemed, but it was quite a few. I knew, and should have remembered, that most of the country, especially in the part of it that I was in, was not like the DFW Metroplex.

Where I lived, there were so many lights on at night, every night, that it was difficult to find a dark spot. Night or day didn't mean anything when driving around DFW. You could see perfectly fine in either case.

But this wasn't DFW. This was the Middle of Nowhere, U.S.A. And out where I was driving, street lights didn't exist.

When nighttime came, and it was dark, it was <u>real</u> dark in places like this, and I had enough experience that I should have known that. But my actions demonstrated that I was absent-minded or stupid or both, and I pressed on, at high speed, into the darkness. I wanted to get home.

***

At freeway speeds, driving into the abyss happens fast. And the abyss came upon me quickly. As I drove, my mind and GPS were calculating how long it would take to get from where I was to where I was going — only I didn't know where I was going.

I was just going further east than I was. I just wanted to make it to the next town with a decent hotel, and then decide how much further to go, if at all.

And it got darker and darker. And the snow came down more and more. And my situation was getting — without me realizing it — more and more perilous.

Though I guess in reality it took some time, it seemed like all of a sudden, I was in it. And the it I was in was not good.

I was slowing down as conditions worsened, but still going fast enough to die. The snow was covering more and more things and my headlights were doing less and less good. There weren't many drivers on the road, but those that were added to the danger. Most of them were semi trucks.

In the last of the light from which I could see, I saw cliffs and ravines — places that no one would drive over in the daylight, or even a normal night, but this was neither. I couldn't see the road. I couldn't see where my lane started and stopped. I couldn't see where the edge of the road ended and off-road, or a ravine, or a cliff started.

I could barely make out the markers indicating the beginning of guardrails designed to keep drivers out of the ravines and away from the drop-offs. Everything was black or white or black covered by white. One thing was indistinguishable from another and terror struck.

For the first time in my life, I was terrified.

I had been scared, anxious, or concerned plenty of times, but this was not that. I had been at a point where I thought I was probably going to die a couple of times in life, and neither of those was anything like this. At both of those times, I was calm and even relaxed. This was the polar opposite.

This was going 60 mph with thousands of pounds of truck and trailer and motorcycle and gear under and around me and essentially doing it with a blindfold on. At any moment, I could go full speed right over a cliff, I could get hit by something, I could hit something. It was unreal. It was surreal. And it was terrifying.

I called my wife in hopes that she would have a suggestion and to let her know the situation that I was in.

"Pull over!"

"I can't...I don't know where the road ends."

"Stop!"

"I can't...I'll get hit by a semi that won't see me or see me in time"

"Go back to Albuquerque!"

"I can't...I don't even see any exits and who knows what would happen if I tried to exit."

I slowed down as much as I felt I safely could. I was shaking with fear and checking my mirrors constantly to look for approaching trucks.

Finally, I saw a sign that said that an exit was ahead. It looked like others had taken it, and I could see some closed businesses at the foot of the exit. As long as I could carefully make it down the exit and across the frontage road, I would live.

I did, and I made it under the overhang of a service station. I stopped the truck and thanked God that that ordeal was over, and that I had not died a horrible death.

Fortunately, my adventure mindset had done a good job of making sure that the cab of my truck was well stocked for such a situation. I had water, snacks, blankets, and plenty of other gear. It would not be an enjoyable or comfortable night, but it would be an adventure.

I told my wife that I was set for the night and would be okay. I think I was even able to top off with fuel at the station, though it was closed, because the pumps still worked.

My wife had been looking to see if there was any lodging that I could get to for the night. She found a small hotel just a couple of exits away, but I didn't think there was any way that getting back out on the freeway made any sense. I was resigned to stay put and just be thankful for safety.

Suddenly, flashing lights appeared. Up, on the freeway, a snowplow was clearing and "salting" the road. I had made it down the exit, if I could just make it back up the on-ramp, I could tuck in right behind the plow truck and have an escort to the exit I needed for the hotel.

I had to make a quick decision and decided that this was God looking out for me. He provided the snowplow. Time to move!

I started the truck and headed for the exit of the service station, ready to cross the road, get on the on-ramp and escape this night of horrors. As I started to go, though, my guardian angel decided to exit — he was done plowing, at least for now.

I started to think all was lost for a better night than a cold one in the truck, when out of nowhere, another snowplow appeared! The Lord will provide. And he did.

Just as the one plow exited, another drove from my right side and made the turn onto the on-ramp as though it was sent just to escort me. In fact, I'm convinced that it was. I got right behind it and it took me right to the exit I needed.

I had never been so happy to check into a hotel in my life. I would have a bed, and television, and hot shower, and all the comforts that this little room could provide. It wasn't heaven, but it wasn't far from it. Thank you God and thank you Sherry!

Chapter Fifteen

ADVENTURE TRAINING CAMP

I made it home the next day. My ankle was still hurting, but I was alive, and had learned a valuable lesson. I would — hopefully — never make that mistake again.

I hobbled around on my left leg for a couple of days. I knew that a doctor had never told me that being able to walk meant that there was no break, but it just seemed like common sense. Many non-doctors had told me that during my life. And besides, I had been wearing motocross boots. Those prevent broken ankles, right?

After a few days, I decided that I needed to get checked out. I went to the best Ortho that I could find to get things looked at.

I knew the drill. I had been X-rayed more times than I could possibly remember in life. I went in the room, did the X-rays and then went to the little room to wait.

A few minutes later, the Doc walked in. "Yeah, you broke your ankle," he said, or words to that effect.

"Huh?...I thought that walking on it meant no break?"

"No, that's not true."

Well, at least I got that resolved.

He asked how I did it, and I told him. I also let him know that I was scheduled to go on another adventure in less than two months.

He let me know that it would take about that long to heal, if I did everything correctly.

"Wait a minute, what?" I said. "Some Dallas Cowboy just broke his ankle and played again in a couple of weeks!"

"Not like this he didn't," said the Doc.

He assured me that the break I had was worse than some ankle breaks. But the good news was that it was not as bad as others. I didn't need surgery or even a cast. I just had to wear a device to keep it immobile for several weeks and not overdo things, and I should be fine. He said that I should be good for the next adventure.

So, Step Five was still a "go."

***

The weeks went by, and I continued my plans to go get fully trained. This adventure would be even more in the middle of nowhere than any other I had had on a bike. And I needed to decide how I would tackle it.

I had gotten hurt on the GSA 1250. I had gotten hurt on the KLR. It seemed only logical that I should "move down the ladder" and use my CRF 250 for this training. It was much lighter than either of those other bikes, and it should allow me to throw it around, when needed.

But, I thought, I will bring my KLR also, just in case something doesn't go as planned. That now seemed to be the "norm" with my adventures, at least it had become my norm.

My ankle healed up, time drew nigh, and the day came to mount up. I had been well prepared for the road trip to Southern California, and this would be a similar distance and along similar roads.

I had the F-350 all loaded with gear, my SPOT GPS devices working — both on the trailer and myself — my CB in the truck, all of my riding safety gear, helmet, etc., and was ready to go.

I loaded and strapped down both the KLR and the CRF. The trailer, like the truck, was a beast. It easily held these two bikes and could have held much, much more.

I headed out.

***

The drive to the place was uneventful, but enjoyable. The instructions for getting to the basecamp for the training were like something out of a mystery novel. A first for me in my biking adventures.

"Once you get to X, go 2.3 miles and look to your right. You should see a green sign with black lettering saying ABC, go down the dirt road to the left of the sign for 9.6 miles and take the Y to the left. From there, go...." And so on.

It warned that there would be no cell coverage, etc., so, follow the directions exactly, and when you get to the gate, do something something something and then proceed like something.

I don't remember any of the details of how it went, but the warnings were welcome and heeded. As I drove closer, the anxiety built.

Another new group of riders to meet — that was supposed to be the good part, I thought. Camaraderie, war stories, friendship, and all that other stuff. I hoped that most if not all would be like me.

It's not that I wanted a bunch of clones of me for companionship sake, but I had just been through two steps where I was in the bottom of the group, or at least felt that way.

The BDR ride was a no-brainer. I was in so far over my head that I had no business riding with that group. The BMW school, I could at least make an argument with myself that I belonged; I had just overstayed my welcome and wasn't smart enough to leave earlier like most of the others to prevent injury.

In preparation for this Training Camp, I watched everything I could and studied the pictures and video available. I desperately wanted to see people who looked like me. I wanted everyone there to be late 50s or over and have a look like they rode, but were not beginners and were not experts.

That's what I felt I was, an in-between, and I didn't want to stand out by having to be dragged along. I don't think I would have minded being the best, but I figured that that was pretty unlikely, so didn't give it much thought.

The videos that I could find showed several guys who looked about my age. And frankly, athletically I felt I was in as good or better shape than any of them. Given that, maybe we were close to the same riding skill level. That's what I told myself to keep the anxiety down.

I found the place, got through the gate, got to the buildings, saw some guys, and figured that I was at the right spot. Someone told me where to park and to come back, check in, and join the group.

Made it. Ready to be trained and for some (mild) adventure.

***

It didn't take long to find out that this group was like many other groups of guys this age that I've encountered. It was a mixed bag. Some of the guys were very friendly and welcoming, and some were distant or a little worse. None, that I recall, were outright rude.

As those of us there sat around outside on a porch, we got to know each other's backgrounds. As the tales were told, my anxiety level rose a bit. For every guy there that seemed to be at my level, there seemed to be at least one, and maybe two, that were former motocross racers.

I made sure to listen carefully, because to me there was a big difference between someone who claimed to have *ridden* motocross and someone who *raced* motocross.

One was a style, in my mind, and one was a breakneck, full-throttle, death-defying activity that I had dreamed about so often, but had never been nearly good enough to think about doing, even if I had had an opportunity.

This mix seemed like it may be a problem for me, but I was there, so I would see how things developed.

At some point that first late afternoon, we all gathered in a rustic meeting room that the base camp facility provided for us to use. We went around the room and formally introduced ourselves and told a little about our background. The first meeting on the porch had been informal and did not involve everyone — this was formal, and involved the Instructors and at least one other "official" of the program whose connection I never did understand.

Virtually everyone there, and especially the Instructors, seemed to be really good guys/gal — there was one female. I anticipated a good week.

There was one other Texan there. He had ridden hard and gotten there on the back of his KTM 1190, I think. It was a bike like the GSA and was certainly powerful enough to take him the mileage that it did, but I think the long, hard ride had worn him out pretty well.

As a part of the group introduction time, the Instructors explained how the week would go. For the first half of the week we would be learning off-road riding, and the second half doing it. It seemed like a good plan, but I had already readied myself for my introduction and attitude toward the course.

My family and I were going on a vacation to Europe a month after this course concluded, and we were going to be there for 30-40 days. My daughter was finishing undergrad at a university in

Sweden, and we would be going to several places during our trip, including the island upon which her university sat. I did not intend to hobble around Europe or have to deal with luggage, a foreign country, and two young boys with a broken arm or worse.

When it got to be my turn to talk about myself, I gave some details of my life and then of my riding background. I talked about having been injured basically my last two times on a bike, and the trip to Europe, and made it clear that I was not at this course to prove anything to anyone. I wanted to learn, if possible, and have some fun and adventure, if I could. But at the first sign of trouble, I would not hesitate to sit out and watch. I was not going to allow myself to get injured again, if there was a way to stop it.

The Instructors said that this class would be conducted under the same "rules" as the BMW school – Challenge by Choice. I had made some bad choices in the past, but intended to take full advantage of the rules this time.

***

The first day of instruction started fine. We did some slow-speed stuff and drove around cones on flat ground, for the most part. I think after that we headed out for a group ride.

I'm pretty sure that this was a little bit of a test, so that the Instructors could see what kind of skills we all had. As at the BDR, the trails that we went on were a diverse collection of "challenges." There were ruts and loose surfaces and tighter surfaces and a little up hill and down, but unlike at the BDR, I don't remember this trail having things on it that would lead to serious injury, unless a big mistake was made or speed was added to the equation.

But of course, that's the next thing that happened. Speed was added.

What I think I figured out was that when groups of riders like this — most if not all better than me — get together and ride on a surface that I can feel comfortable with at my skill level, they often want to add the element that will take matters out of my comfort zone.

Figuring out how to negotiate a rut that zigs and zags can be done with some practice, but figuring it out at high speed reduces the margin of error. It's really as simple as this — you are less likely to fall at slow speeds, and if you do, you are less likely to get seriously injured. Well, maybe.

Given that I had fallen at the Performance Center at slow speed and ended up in the hospital seemed to blow that theory out of the water. But still, had I taken that same fall at a higher speed, the injuries would almost certainly have been worse.

Whatever. I couldn't and can't figure it all out. All I know is that it was all I could do to negotiate the trails and roads that we were on at moderate speeds. Once the group wanted to take it up a notch, I had to fall back.

Still, my ego was fine. I didn't care if the group took off without me. I could find my way back to the campsite, and would rather be there without injuries.

Dinner on the first night was nice, it was prepared by the owners of the place where we were staying, and it was perfect for this kind of group. The weather was awesome, and the group that I had been assigned to bunk with was good.

I think there were 4 or 5 of us in one big cabin, and then others were spread out in groups of two or three in other structures.

The next day, I think we started with some slow stuff and then headed for tougher terrain. The Instructors announced that we were going to learn sand and rocky terrain. Neither of those sounded like anything that I wanted to do at the time, but I reserved judgement until I saw the terrain.

We got to a medium-sized uphill that was very rocky. This was not like an uphill that had a couple of big rocks here and there; this was an uphill that had rocks of various sizes everywhere.

To any skilled off-road rider, this may not have been much of a challenge, but for me, it was another broken bone waiting to happen. I passed.

The Instructors were understanding of my situation and gave me their thoughts. But my sense was that as nice as they were, these Instructors were not of the same caliber as the BMW School. As mentioned previously, there, careful instruction was given about body position, weighting, what-ifs, etc. Here, it seemed the style was more like, "Hey, we're gonna ride up these rocks — watch how I do it and do it like me."

Again, I was the odd man out. I think maybe one other rider passed on that challenge, but I'm not even sure of that — and didn't care.

I was just enjoying being there to the extent I could, and would get in riding in a new state that I had rarely been to, to the extent I could. If it was a lot less than the others, so be it.

The next day, the group did something, but I don't even recall what they went off to learn. Instead of joining them, I decided that I would go for rides on paved roads and gravelly hard-packed roads in the area on which I felt comfortable. It was a good day and I enjoyed the rides, and didn't miss the lessons.

So far, so good — I don't think that anyone had gotten hurt in those first few days. That night, it was time for the briefing of the extended ride that would comprise the second half of the course.

The Instructor told us about the route. He said that we would head out on public roads, but that at some point, we would turn onto and spend a great deal of time on some type of restricted land.

He explained that since we were riding as a group, there was a chance that we would get stopped by some type of official and possibly asked some questions. As he described what may happen, it was clear to me that we were being asked to cross a line that I was not willing to cross.

I already had serious concerns about going on the extended ride. It seemed clear that I would not be able to keep up, and thus would either slow everyone down or have to bail out at some point. And given the route, the options for bailing out did not seem good.

Now, with this new information and instruction, the decision was made. I would do my own thing.

I had paid for the week, including all of the accommodations, so I wanted to use those until I had squeezed all the fun out of the week that I could. I consulted the map with the Instructor and told him that I would start and do the public roads with them up to a point, then I would bail out and just meet them at that first night of lodging.

***

Once I announced — or let it be known — that I was not going to go with the group, the female in the class said that she didn't feel capable of doing the intended ride either. She had done much better than me so far in the course, in terms of keeping up with the curriculum, but she had reached her limit. She did not want to get caught out in the middle of the long ride and *then* decide to bail, because she knew that would put her on her own in the middle of nowhere.

It was fine by me for her to ride with me that next day, and we would meet up with the group at the end of the day.

The next morning started fine. Everyone was fired up for the trip. We had breakfast, then assembled for a group photo, and then lined up to get ready to take off.

I decided that it would make much more sense for me to ride the KLR than the 250, since I was going to be on paved roads and highways, or at least well-maintained public roads. As it turned out, I am very glad that I did.

We took off from the basecamp, and pretty much from the beginning, the leader decided that he was going to make "good time." I don't know that I would say that the pace was "shot out of a cannon" — like it had been at the BDR event, but we were moving. I don't think there is any way that the 250 could have kept up.

We rode together throughout a portion of the morning, and then it got to be time for the group to take off on their off-road adventure. We had already decided where we would meet up, so our twosome went one way, and the group went the other.

The Instructors made it clear that I was on my own — or we were on our own — once we split up, and that they could not be "responsible" for us. That didn't matter, since I don't know that anyone could hold them accountable for anything that happened at the course anyway.

Once we went our own way, we had a great time. We rode through some amazing parts of America that a great many people never see, and got to stop at some very interesting historical spots and markers.

This was my first time realizing that there is a big difference between riding on an adventure like this solo and doing it with another person or group.

Though I had done plenty of group rides in the past, they always had a destination that was really the only point of the ride. They were not just to explore. I found that when exploring, it is much easier to not be encumbered with another rider whose wishes need to be considered.

To be clear, it was not that the two of us did not get along perfectly well, or that either of us complained about anything.

Rather, it was a matter of the anxiety of being worried about being an irritant to the other person.

Often, I would see something and want to stop, or go back to something that I had seen a mile or so back. What that meant was having to signal my intentions, if I decided to do that. But more often, what it meant was missing out on what I wanted to do for fear of creating a dangerous situation by trying to signal the stop and doing a U-Turn or irritating my companion.

Regardless, the day went well. It was hot, and we stopped at some remote locations to get some Gatorade or the like and take short breaks, but other than that, the day was uneventful.

Late in the day, we met up with the group at the pre-arranged rendezvous spot. Here was another instance of something not being exactly right. I don't remember the details, but it had something to do with us going through some entry point and whether we did it according to whatever "rules" there were.

We got to the hotel all together and got paired up for the night, and told what time and where to meet for dinner. That's when we would hear their war stories — and they had some to tell.

***

The rider that I got paired up with for the night was a really nice guy, and we got settled in our room. After showers, etc., we headed for dinner. By then, thanks to my roommate, I had already heard about some of the problems the group had had.

One of the riders that I met that first day — the only other Texan in the class — had taken a bad fall. He was a former motocross racer, so I knew things had to have been intense.

He was not hospitalized, but had injured his leg so badly that he could not ride.

From what I was told, the group was on a rutted route that was challenging, and was pushing the throttles hard. As with any real rutted surface — not the "training ruts" of the BMW Performance Center — the ruts do what nature has allowed or forced them to do. They vary from deeper to shallower to wider to narrower and change directions at will.

Once in one, the challenge can be how to get out, if you need to get out at a certain point. Apparently, the Texan was in a rut and moving at a good clip when he tried to get out of it. As he did, the bike did not cooperate and down he went, hard. Luckily for him, to some extent, he was on a rented bike. Though his big KTM Adventure bike had gotten him from Texas to the Camp, it was apparently too big for the kind of riding that he anticipated during the course. Or maybe he just realized that if he crashed, it would be better to do it on a rented bike. Either way, the good news was that his big bike was okay — except that now he couldn't ride it.

As things turned out, I found out at dinner that the Texan's bad luck was good luck for another rider who had had bad luck, as well.

In his case, it wasn't that he was injured, but his bike was. This rider had not done like the Texan; he had not rented a bike. Instead, he used his beautiful new Triumph Adventure Bike for the whole course — or at least until it wouldn't run anymore.

I don't recall the exact story of how he had done it, but the Triumph rider had somehow managed to jam something into something and that made something jam into his radiator. Whatever all the jamming was, what it meant was that he had a bike that stopped working mid-ride. He was in the middle of nowhere that day, with a bike that no longer worked. Fortunately, he was with the group.

Since the Texan had only put himself out of commission but not his rented bike, and the Triumph rider had only put his bike out of commission, but not himself, Triumph Man was able to take over the rental of Texan's bike. Of course, his bike was still out of commission out in the middle of nowhere.

As luck would have it, the people from the basecamp operation were able to come to nowhere and rescue the bike. That was the good part of the luck. The bad part of it was that since even to them nowhere was not right around the corner, and they were a commercial operation, there would be a charge. As I recall, it cost Triumph man about $400.00 just to get his bike brought from nowhere to basecamp, and of course that still left the bike far from true civilization.

***

I listened to all of the stories of the broken bike, the broken rider, and all the other "fun" that the group had had without me (and my riding companion), and decided that the fun had pretty much been squeezed from this event.

I was at the end of my Five Step Plan, or at least so close to it that the end was in sight. I think there was one more night in a hotel that I had paid for and one more day of independent riding and then hooking up with the group that I could do, but I decided that it was time for me to call a personal end to the operation. I was done, ready to get home, rethink my adventure biking, and get rested and ready for Europe.

I don't remember what my riding companion did, but I don't think she headed back with me. The next morning, I got up and headed for basecamp. My plan the entire day of riding was get to basecamp, load up as fast as possible, and head home. And get there as fast as I could.

***

My memory is that I had been told either at dinner the night before or at breakfast that morning that the Injured Texan was headed back to basecamp also. There was no reason for him to stick with the group in the chase vehicle, and he was hurting pretty badly. He just wanted to get home too.

He had a much bigger problem than me, though. He couldn't ride, and did not have a vehicle other than his big KTM to get home on. The nearest airport of any size was quite a distance away, and his home was hundreds of miles or more away. He was in a fix.

The entire day of riding, I organized my plan in my mind. I would get to basecamp, drive straight to my truck and trailer, load up without saying anything to anyone, and then with not much more than a wave, I would be on the road.

The NBA Finals were going on. I was hooked on sports, and I wanted to watch the game that night. I did not want to talk to anyone; I wanted to be left alone, and I just wanted to enjoy the drive in solitude, get to a hotel early enough to watch the game, settle in, and relax.

I was 100% selfish.

There was another rider who needed help. I was from the same state as him. I lived within a couple hundred miles or so from where he needed to go, but who cares. This was all about me. Besides, I already had two bikes in my trailer, and I couldn't fit three. Sorry.

"Semper Fi — Hurray for me and forget about you." That was the comical rendition of the Marine Corps slogan. In the Corps, that version was joked about, but used as an insult to any Marine who would have anything like that attitude on even the smallest of things.

But this wasn't the Marines. And he wasn't a fellow Marine. And I was tired, and I didn't owe him anything.

***

The day's riding was uneventful. I don't think I stopped for anything other than maybe fuel. I just wanted to get back. And I did.

I made it to basecamp and began to execute the plan.

Throughout the day, playing in my head were all of the lessons I had learned as a child. I had been raised in a Christian home by the best possible parents. My dad was a Baptist Pastor and my mom was the Minister of Education in the church.

I don't remember ever not knowing that I was called to "Do unto others" as I would have them "do unto me." I knew that as a Christian, I was to help others. I was to do more than respond if asked, I was to seek out needs and meet them when I could.

I was a Christian, wasn't I? It's okay if I leave my fellow man stranded hundreds of miles from home and injured, isn't it? I had things that I wanted to do. And surely even the Good Samaritan wouldn't try to figure out a way to get three bikes back home with a two-bike trailer — and a pickup truck.

I made it to my trailer. I got it opened and the bike loaded. All I needed to do was get out of there and get far enough away that my conscience would shut up.

Whether I was required to "check out" or not, I don't recall, but somehow I know I interacted with the folks that ran the basecamp — and with the Injured Texan. It was okay. He had a plan. He would leave his bike there. He would pay someone to give him a ride to an airport, where he could buy a ticket home, and he would go home and recuperate. Once he was well enough, he would fly back out, somehow get a ride to the basecamp, and ride his bike home — oh, and he would pay the basecamp folks to store his bike for however many weeks or months it took him to get back.

"Sounds good to me! See ya!" And I started driving away.

But my conscience would not shut up. What was worse, I tried to make myself feel better by putting on some Christian music. Surely having that on while I drove away would give God a good reason to excuse me for being such a jerk, and dishonoring the name of Christ, while I walked past the injured man on the road and left him for a Samaritan to deal with.

I think I made it less than a mile before I felt like Jonah after he was spit out of the whale. I found a spot wide enough and turned the truck and trailer around.

As I drove up, thoroughly embarrassed at what a jackass I had been for driving away in the first place, the Texan and others asked what I was doing back there. I said that I thought that we could figure something out and get the Texan and his bike, along with my two bikes, home.

He told me not to worry about it, but at that point, there was no way I was going to wrestle God for the entire drive and the rest of my life. I let the Texan know that we were doing it.

***

The Texan's bike was big and the KLR was not petite. So they would have to go in the trailer. But, other than the fact that I had the entire bed filled with gear, there was no reason that the Honda could not fit in the bed of the truck. I wasn't necessarily smart enough to figure out how to tie it in myself, but there were others there that could, so we did.

It took an hour or so to get everything rearranged and loaded and tied down, but within an hour or two, we were off. I would miss the NBA game, or at least most of it, and wouldn't have the solitude that I thought I had wanted, but I also wouldn't forever have to know what a jerk I could be. And I could help a fellow biker who really needed help.

We hit the roads, backroads, dirt roads, and eventually made it to highways and then finally a freeway. I know that we made amazingly good time, and I enjoyed the company. We drove as far as we could, having left relatively late in the afternoon, and made it to some hotel somewhere. If we pushed it, we could probably make it to my house the next day.

***

We got up on Day 2 of the trip and took off. I don't remember where we started that morning, but we ended at my house in DFW. We were both exhausted, and decided that it would be better to rest for the night, prior to heading to his house, a couple hundred miles south.

The next day was thankfully uneventful, as the entire trip home had been. It was a few hours to get the Texan to his home and unloaded and dropped off, and then a few hours' drive back to my house, but once I was back home, I could fully relax.

I had made it. I had made it through all five parts of the plan, but unfortunately, I now knew that I was not the Adventure Rider that I had set out to be. I felt woefully unprepared to even think about going on any of the International Adventures that had piqued my interest in all of this. But at least as I drove, sat there, or whatever, contemplating my situation, I wasn't in a hospital or doctor's office.

And, I had learned a great deal. I had learned many lessons along my way, and having that knowledge would help me wherever my biking took me in the future.

Chapter Sixteen

LESSONS LEARNED

S o, what all had I learned? I tried to make mental notes as I went, and over the years since the beginning of the Adventure Journey, I have written notes to myself in various places. Here, in no particular order are some of the things that I learned — and wish I had known ahead of my Journey:

1. Yes, you can break your ankle wearing Motocross Boots: I had always wondered this. In fact, I guess that I assumed that that was the point of those big, stiff, cumbersome boots. If they couldn't stop your ankle from twisting in a way that would lead to a break, what was the point? Well, obviously, the point is that they do protect your lower leg and foot and ankle, but no, they do not absolutely prevent ankle (and assumedly other) breaks. I know, because I did it.

2. You can walk with a broken ankle. Notwithstanding what

I was told as a kid, a broken bone does not necessarily render a limb inoperable. I walked on my broken ankle for several days — and rode with it briefly — before I knew that it was broken. And a broken ankle is not a broken ankle is not a broken ankle; there are different kinds of breaks, so just because you or a friend has had a broken ankle (or whatever) in the past, it does not mean that a current injury is the same as the past one.

3. You can ride a motorcycle and shift gears with a broken ankle, assuming that you have on proper footwear. I suppose you could do it with bare feet and the back of your bare heel, if you were tough enough, but I don't want to try. In fact, I'm hoping to never have the pleasure of doing it with boots on again, but it's good to know that you can.

4. Rib Protectors exist. I had known from at least my teen years about Motocross torso protectors. In fact, I had owned one or more and bought some for my kids. But I guess I did not even contemplate that there was a way to protect your ribs, if you were not wearing a Motocross outfit. As it turns out, there is. And it's really easy, and not very expensive. It's sad to think that all of my misery — and my wife's — at the end of the BMW Performance Center could have been avoided by a relatively inexpensive piece of hard rubber/plastic that straps on under a jacket and is held in place by a couple of straps and some Velcro,

but not as sad as it will be if I allow something like that to happen to me again because I'm too lazy to wear protective gear that I now know exists.

5. <u>Never</u> ride a bike without having a charger (and a long cord) with you. You never know when you will end up in a hospital, if you are on a motorcycle. And while you would think that any slightly kind person working in a hospital would help you get a charger when you desperately need one, that is not true. The world is made up of all kinds, and you can't count on being able to find a charger, when you need one, if you don't have one with you. Also, have long cords with you, to the extent that you can. Your charger may have to be plugged in quite a distance from you, if you are having to lay in bed, due to injuries.

6. Have backup plans figured out ahead of time. You need to know how you are going to get home if you can't ride — or if you can't fly. You need to have thought of what you will do if you are injured such that you can't take care of yourself and are away from home. And you need to have thought of how you will get your bike home if it is wrecked or you can't ride it home.

7. You need to have a backup plan for friends abandoning you. It's easy to think through and commit that you won't leave an injured friend — and you would think that you could count on your friends to do the same. But what if

they are injured first and then they leave, and *then you* get injured. Think through how your "buddy system" is going to work ahead of time and have a contingency plan.

8. Know who you are trusting to take you on a trip. I'm not sure how you would go about asking a commercial guide whether they intend to ask you to do things during the trip that you are not willing to do, but there must be some way. It would definitely be a good idea to find out exactly where the trip is going to be going, and who owns the areas that you will be crossing. From there, with the help of the internet, hopefully you could find answers as to what is allowed and what is prohibited — and then ask questions from there.

9. Always have your insurance card with you — and have good insurance. That means both vehicle insurance and medical insurance. That is just good advice to anyone who is riding a motorcycle anywhere and anytime, and probably just all-around good advice for everyone.

10. You will crash. They told us that at the beginning of the Performance Course, and it turned out to be true. From my experience, does everyone riding off-road crash on every ride? No, thankfully. But given what happened to the Texan, years of experience do not make any of us immune. So, count on crashing, and be as ready for it as possible.

11. Riding off road and Off-Road Riding are two separate things. Okay, so I don't know exactly how to say that. But here's what I mean: Just because you have ridden motorcycles in places that were not roadways, does not mean that you have what the experts consider "Off-Road Riding Experience." What they actually mean may be as varied as who is saying it. But, clearly, riding around on flat surfaces that have good grip at slow speeds is not the same thing as flying down a trail that is rutted, has rocks of various sizes, has drop offs, has sandy spots, has gravelly spots — you get the idea.

12. Hard-sided Panniers can be very dangerous. Fortunately for me, I did not get to find out first hand exactly how dangerous Hard Panniers can be, but having taken the fall that I did, immediately after being warned to remove my very hard panniers, I can envision pretty well what would have happened to my leg. It would not have been pretty. I will never ride off road with hard-sided panniers, though I know that other riders do.

13. You do not have to spend a fortune to get decent gear. I have now taken a great many trips and a great many falls, all while wearing my very inexpensive jacket and pants. In my opinion, they still look almost like new — and perform like new also. I would never advise someone who is just thinking about figuring out if they like Adventure

Riding to go out and buy the top of the market stuff. Some things shouldn't be skimped on, but for most items you should at least check the less expensive stuff, to see if it will get the job done.

14. As for whether to Rent or Bring Your Own Bike, the lesson is not clear. Both options come with risks. At the immersion course, it was not clear what a rider would have to pay if he trashed a rented bike, but it certainly was not clear that that was "included in the price," the way it was at the Performance Center. On the flip side, Triumph Man did substantial damage to his bike, it appeared — so now he would have to pay *and* be without his bike for some time *and* have a damaged/repaired bike going forward. Had he just similarly damaged a rented bike, he would only have the cost of repairing the rental bike to deal with, if that.

15. To my knowledge, there is no license required universally to hold yourself out as someone who acts as a Motorcycle Guide. To a large extent, it is *caveat emptor* — let the buyer beware. To illustrate the point, one of the more minor things that I did when going through my steps was attend a minor Motorcycle Show that was local to me. As a part of it, there were speakers on various topics. I listened to one "very experienced" Tour Operator talk about how he led a group into a very treacherous area and either had

or almost had a "client" drive off a cliff in the dark, when trying to get from one area to another, after the plan had gone awry. I crossed him off my "Operators to Tour With" list.

16. There are different levels of protection for body armor. This is one of those things that I just learned. I assumed that it was all in the cost of the original gear, but what I discovered recently is that I could replace the relatively light body armor in my bargain jacket and pants with top-of-the-line (rating-wise) body armor. Will it make a difference if I crash? The laws of physics say, Yes.

17. Modern technology really is better. Okay, maybe to a point — I have no interest in being in a self-driving car, when my GPS is wrong all the time. But, there is no question that my GSA 1250 is far superior to my lovably nostalgic KLR. The braking, the driver information available on the TFT Display, the ergonomics, the cruise control, the traction control, the various modes available, etc., etc. When you have a choice, go with the more technologically advanced bike — the extra 100 pounds is not what's going to do you in.

18. Photos and videos can be deceiving — or not tell the whole story. Yes, those old guys in the photos may be old, but they may also be former Motocross Racers. They may not look like they are in the best physical shape of their

lives, but they may have forgotten more about motorcycling than most people will ever know. And the terrain that the experts in the videos make look easy and fun may be nearly impossible and a huge pain, at best, to a lesser rider.

19. One person's description of a ride or terrain may not fit another person's reality. If a rider tells you that a particular route is going to be easy, even if he or she is telling you the gospel truth in their mind, it does not mean that you will find the route to be easy. The weather may have changed, the route may have changed, and your skill set may not be what the other rider's skill set is.

20. Motorcyclists are no different than the general population. Some are friendly and helpful, some are very friendly and helpful, and some are not. It is no safer to make assumptions about people just because they ride a motorcycle than it is to make them about anyone else in society.

The Final Lesson is the one that I learned and am living now: It's okay to be the kind of Adventure Rider that's right for YOU. I'm now 63. I was in my late 50s when I started down the Adventure path. It's not clear to me that I ever had the skill set to learn to be the kind of Adventure Rider that I thought I wanted to be, but it's certain that I will never be that now. And I don't care. The path that I'm on now is exactly the one that I'm supposed to be on, and I love it.

CHAPTER SEVENTEEN

CMA AND BEYOND

I n the spring of 2020, the world changed and pretty much shut down for a long time. Shortly after the shutdown hit, my wife and I decided that it was time to make a major change in life.

It was time to move from our five acres in DFW, and find a bigger place. And a place that was away from all of the craziness in the cities.

God brought us to a place that is as close to Heaven as anywhere I've ever been — Nocona, Texas.

Nocona is in what some call the North Texas Hill Country. From a motorcyclist's perspective the roads around Nocona are amazing. They are almost all in fantastic shape, and they have lots and lots of curves and elevation changes and beautiful scenery that they wind through.

Moreover, there are an endless number of dirt roads, gravel roads, and paved roads that turn into dirt or gravel roads.

When we moved here in 2020, I still had my Harley CVO Road Glide — which was beautiful — and my KLR and CRF. Of those three, it was really only the KLR that I found to be well-suited for this part of Texas.

Many of the roads surrounding Nocona do not have shoulders, or at least not much of a shoulder. Some of the roads are too narrow to easily and safely do a U-Turn with a full-sized Harley. And virtually all of the roads have fairly high speed limits.

There are no freeways for miles, but the highways have 75 mile per hour speed limits, and the CRF simply can't handle that speed. It can get to 75 with me on it, but probably not without a steep and long downhill.

The Harley — at least for me — was too easily blown around on the shoulder-less roads, for my liking. So, the KLR was really the only one of the three that worked well around the area. But of course it was the same KLR whose technology and ergonomics I found to be generally lacking.

***

After being here long enough that I felt like I had thoroughly explored the area, I decided that it was time for a big motorcycling change. The Harley had to go. I needed to have, as my primary ride, the best bike that I had found for the types of riding that I would be doing, and that was the GSA.

Despite having been injured the last time I was on one, I knew what an amazing bike the GSA was. I knew that it could handle roads with high speeds and sudden off-road challenges better than any bike I had ever seen, so the move was made.

I sold the Road Glide back to the Harley dealership and promptly took that money and bought a GSA 1250. This bike was not only as good as the one I had been injured on, it was improved.

What I came to find out was that the riding position of the GSA was as comfortable as any bike that I had ever ridden, and wind tolerance was far superior to any Harley that I had ever owned. As for it's speed and quickness, I'm not sure that it could be matched by anything that I had ever been on, except maybe the FJ, since it was almost a literal rocket.

We moved to Nocona in the Fall of 2020, and by early Fall of 2021, I had the GSA. What I knew I needed to do immediately was head to the Performance Center and kill off the Ghost of Injuries Past. I had no fear of the GSA, but I did have a healthy respect for how easily it could take you from good times to bad. I wanted to at least have more confidence on it.

I had a trip that I needed to make to the East Coast in September 2021 anyway, and that gave me the perfect opportunity. This time, though, instead of being with a group, I would book a Private Lesson.

As luck would have it, my lesson was booked with one of the best GSA riders in the World and a person that would become a lifelong friend — Ricardo Rodriguez.

At the school, Ricardo took me back through the challenges that I had done before, but also helped me to conquer some of the ones that we hadn't gotten to, or that I had chosen to skip. By the time

I left that day, I was far from an expert, but I knew much more about my bike and had much more confidence on it.

I decided that my first true Adventure on my new bike would be riding it up to the Evel Knievel Museum in Topeka, Kansas. Evel was a childhood hero, and I was one of those kids who always wanted, but never got, the Evel Knievel wind-up toy that did real motorcycle jumps and crashed a lot — just like the real guy.

I had ridden the bike some by trailering it on my trip to the East Coast and taking it out in a few places, but that did not feel like a real Adventure. This first adventure trip to the museum and Kansas did.

I got to an unexpected dirt road or two on the trip and faced weather that was below freezing. My gear and the bike worked flawlessly in all of that, and the trip was the first one of any significant length on a bike that I had actually enjoyed from start to finish.

Something else had happened to me prior to that first Adventure, though, and that led to my next adventures and the ones I hope to have from now until I can't ride anymore. I became a new person.

***

I had been raised Baptist. I was blessed with the two best adoptive parents that anyone could ever ask for, and they had raised me in the church.

That upbringing put me in a position wherein I'm not sure that I can ever remember not knowing about God, or his son Jesus. By age 10, I had been baptized and could say the books of the Bible a couple of times to a burning match. I could pass any basic Bible knowledge quiz.

But, something was missing. It was very missing. And I didn't know what it was.

In college, I had sought God. It wasn't that I needed more information on him; rather, I wanted to really encounter him. In fact, my motorcycle played a part in my search.

Some Sundays, instead of going to church, I would take my King James Bible and ride my DT 175 out to a place in Waco called Cameron Park. I would sit by myself at a picnic table with my Bible and read and pray and try to understand God and hear from him about what he wanted from me, who he really was, and seek help with all the confusing things that an 18 year old thinks about.

In the Marine Corps, I had sought God, in much the same way. When I was out in the desert, I would read the little military-issue King James version Bible that I had and pray and contemplate and try to find God's Will for my life. Throughout all of that, though, and even more so in law school, I had the "Christian me" and the "Real me," and they weren't the same.

I could flip the switch and play Religion, or not.

In the years after law school, my life changed with divorces, kids, etc., and I tried a great many things to find what I was missing. None of it worked.

One of the things I tried was motorcycling. I rode with the Leathernecks, and hung out with various bikers. Just like everything else, though, that did not fill the hole inside me.

I can remember seeing something about the Christian Motorcyclist Association, and I even thought that maybe that would be the place I would find my answers. Except that presented one serious problem.

If I was going to hang out with a group like that, I would have to swear off (pun intended) all the "fun" parts of motorcycling. I would have to have the Religion Switch flipped all the time. Yuck. That was of no interest.

It's not that I was anywhere close to a 1%'er — far from it. I had no interest in criminal activity. But I didn't want to not be able to be "cool" and hang out at places like Strokers in Dallas and with the kind of people that hang out there. It's not a bad crowd — or it wasn't back when I used to go — but it is a normal "Worldly" crowd. There are plenty of skimpily clad young ladies and plenty of language and plenty of drinking. It was just a non-stop party.

If I started rubbing elbows with CMA and their ilk, surely ever being able to be anywhere "fun" would end.

***

When we moved to Nocona, we decided that we would give church a try again. We committed to the idea that we would find and get involved in a local church. More importantly, though, I committed to the idea that I would find God, once and for all.

A lifetime of looking, off and on, and searching for peace in other places and in other things and in other people, was going to come to an end. If I couldn't find him in the Bible, he couldn't be found, I reasoned. And I set out on my journey.

I discovered a new translation of the Bible called the Christian Standard Bible, and got a copy of it to start reading. From years of Bible study growing up, I knew that I needed to start in the New Testament.

I believed in God. I believed in Jesus. So what was I missing?

We found a church, then felt led to go to another one closer to our home, and fell in love with it. As I learned more and more in my personal reading and study, I also learned more as I took over the leadership role in our Sunday School class.

In conjunction with all of that, I found a great many podcasts to listen to, and YouTube videos to watch.

Then, one night, I came across a video entitled Paul Washer's Shocking Sermon. I can't do it justice in a few words, but it laid out that if you claim the title Christian, but act like the non-Christian World, you probably shouldn't claim the title of Christian. That concept started to resonate, but it made no sense.

I had been told my whole life that as long as I "believed," I was "in." I was saved. And I was told that "once saved, always saved."

Then one day, on a podcast, I heard a preacher talking about Unconverted Believers. "Hey! Maybe we're onto something here," I thought.

I believed, but didn't feel like I had ever been converted. I didn't have a "new heart." I wasn't a "new creation." So, I dug deeper.

I found that "believe" could also be translated from the Greek as "trust." That made sense That finally clicked.

Then, one day, it happened. I can't tell you the day, or the day of the week, or the time. But it happened. I was finally reconciled to God, and my life began again.

We ended up finding another church in our town, and I am convinced that we were led there so that we could meet Tom Jenkins, a lifelong motorcyclist, also.

As my wife and I went to Sunday School that first week, Tom was our Sunday School teacher. And as he introduced himself, he did it with his CMA business card. Tom and his wife, Brenda, were founders of the local CMA Chapter.

At first, I wasn't sure that I was interested in CMA, not for the same reasons as before, but just because I had enough on my plate in life. One day, though, CMA was having a short ride and gathering, and I felt led to attend.

What I found was a really good group of people and fellow Christians who enjoyed bikes and riding. As I dug further into the group, I found mottos that resonated with me — the new me:

Riding for the Son

Changing the world, one heart at a time, and

We are here if you need us

That was it! Now it all made sense!

God had blessed me more than I could have ever imagined possible. As a part of that, he had given me resources to allow me to have multiple bikes, and a great truck and trailer. I wanted to ride for him, I wanted to help change the world for the better, and I had the resources available to help motorcyclists when needed.

This was it. This was my motorcycle Adventure calling. This was why God had put the love of motorcycles in my heart.

***

Since joining CMA, I have been able to go on two rides that I consider to be Mission Trips. Both were Adventures — of the best kind.

The first Adventure was one that when I took off, I wasn't sure where I was headed or for how long. I was anxious to go, had the time to go, and was even partially packed. But I didn't have a destination figured out, and couldn't even decide on a direction.

My wife said, "Just take off and see where God leads you." So, I did.

I left Nocona and headed East on Highway 82. As I rode, I thought of places that I would like to ride that were to the East, if only I had a chance. And now I did.

I had always dreamed of going on a long trip, and this was my opportunity.

The GSA ran flawlessly. It was perfect for the highways and backroads and occasional Freeways that I would end up on. I headed for the home of one of my best friends from the Marines, who lived in Northern Mississippi. After a night there, I decided that this was my chance to do some riding in Florida that I had missed out on back in the 1980s, so I headed that way.

Before getting to my home State, I had a chance to stop in Southern Alabama, make some new friends, and see some family that I rarely got to see.

Along the way, with my CMA vest prominently displayed and witnessing tracts, cards, and coins ready to hand out, I looked for opportunities to meet people. Day after day, I would meet people and talk and discuss whatever came up, but at the end of pretty much every day, I felt like I had missed out on so many opportunities to witness.

Nevertheless, as the trip continued, I made some new lifelong friends, and continued to my old home, in Florida. It felt very cathartic to be heading home — coming full circle. I would ride back where I had first ridden the first bikes that I ever had.

The Adventure was the trip. I didn't look for any challenging terrain, and I'm not even sure that I encountered any dirt roads. What I did see and do, though, was reconnect with old friends, see family, make new friends, and see some things that I had wanted to see my entire life, but had never taken the time.

I finally made it to St. Augustine, a place that I had always known about, but for some reason had never gotten to. I went from there to the Fountain of Youth, and walked where some of America's earliest explorers had walked. I drank from the Fountain of Youth and tried to soak in everything I could of the experiences that I was having.

As I was preparing to head back toward Texas, a friend asked me to try to go by and witness to his brother. He told me that his brother needed Jesus, and that maybe I could connect with him and break down some barriers. I was still relatively new to this whole mission thing and trying to share my faith in a more detailed way, but prayed for the right words and was willing to give it a try.

I found the house and was met with severe resistance. It was clear that my message was not wanted, and that I was viewed as somewhat of an intruder upon their solitude, just by being there and saying "Hi," and asking to pray with them.

I felt sad for them, but climbed back on my GSA and headed out. I wasn't going to let their attitude diminish the Adventure that I was on.

I don't remember a great deal about the trip back to Texas. But overall, the entire experience was the kind of Adventure that I had always wanted to take. I know that I stopped in Destin, Florida, and did some Scuba diving while on it and was much more blessed by the people that I met along the way, than I was able to bless.

I got back home to Nocona exhausted. It had been somewhere close to three weeks in all that I was gone, I think, and I had enjoyed every minute of it.

***

A lot happened between that first big trip and my second one. Before the first one, I had been hospitalized with Guillain-Barré syndrome (GBS), but had recovered. Before the second, I had another bout of GBS.

In addition to all of that, work and home life got busy, and before I knew it, another year of life had flown by. I had several goals after each bout of GBS, and motorcycling was a part of them.

I wanted to engage in all of the activities that I loved again, partly because getting older is a reality, and partly to prove to myself that I could still do them. Scuba diving, snow skiing, and motorcycling are the Big Three for me at this point in my life, along with working out in all the various forms I love.

It was now 2025, and I had hit all the others after the last bout. It was time for a trip. I was aching to go.

I had been wanting to ride to Dodge City, Kansas, for a long time. I grew up watching all the cowboy shows and wanted to be a cowboy my entire life in the same way that I would love to be in law enforcement — I am drawn to the ideas, but they have never fit into my life's plan.

Nevertheless, I wanted to go see where all the romantic tales of the Old West took place. Dodge City was one of those, and Tombstone, Arizona, was another. That, I thought, would make a great trip.

So, the planning began. This would be a great opportunity to see things I've always wanted to see, enjoy some adventurous riding, and connect with people on behalf of CMA to share the Gospel and talk to them about Jesus.

***

I set out in February of 2025 and the riding was at first all that I could have asked for. The weather was great, and the BMW was operating like a dream.

I didn't have a specific agenda, but basically just had Dodge and Tombstone as my intended destinations, and I would see what else I could fit in along the way.

Several years earlier, my family and I had stumbled across a Billy the Kid Museum in New Mexico, but it was closing right as we arrived. I was not a huge Billy the Kid fan, but knew that he was a central figure in the Old West sagas. So, I added that stop to the tentative agenda too.

I made it to Dodge City and the Boot Hill Casino at the end of Day Two. The stay was not really at the Casino, but rather at the Hilton property attached to it. It was a little out of the way, but just the name of the place was enough to make it the right fit.

The next day I toured Dodge City and it was every bit or more than what I hoped it would be. The entire experience was awesome, and it just made me want more.

I took plenty of photos and finished the day by riding out to the remnants of the markings of the Santa Fe Trail. There was not a great deal to see of it, but just being there was worth the experience. I stood on some high ground and tried to get any sense of what the brave people who had blazed through the area two hundred years earlier had felt.

The next morning, I rode once more around Dodge City wanting to feel the feel as best I could then I set out in the general direction of Billy the Kid's old stomping grounds. I couldn't get there in one day, or didn't want to, which meant that I would be stopping somewhere in Texas that night.

That was the only part of the trip that felt particularly odd.

It felt a little like being a kid who wants the great adventure of camping out but sets up in the backyard and goes inside to ask mom for help with the marshmallows. But geography being what it is, I didn't see a lot of choice, so I settled on just not memorializing it with any photos.

It did give me a chance, though, to figure out my next couple of destinations. I knew that there was a lot of Wild West history between Dodge City and Tombstone; I just had to find it.

I don't remember who, but someone I met on the trip to Dodge City told me about going to the actual site of the Billy the Kid jailbreak and Billy's grave. That sounded like a must-do.

Along the way, I found out about the Dalton Gang Hideout also being available to tour. I wasn't exactly sure who the Dalton Gang was, but I had heard of them, and I didn't want to miss the chance to see any part of Wild West history that I could.

The riding was just riding those days, except that I did get to experience being alone on my steed, and the beginnings of being really alone on it that would come in the next several days. The only concern I ever had was dropping the bike.

I knew from my days at the Performance Center that I could not get the bike up myself – or was about 90% sure that I couldn't. And I didn't want to test it.

I wasn't looking to do any off-roading or anything else to increase my chances of dropping the bike, but simple things like the roads near the Dalton Gang hideout and the terrain – a sizeable hill – mixed with slow speed riding caused me some anxiety.

Nevertheless, the touring of the Hideout, then the Billy the Kid Museum, then Fort Sumner was all fantastic.

Fort Sumner is a well-preserved village with lots of original buildings, including the Courthouse from which Billy escaped. The museum there is one of the best that I have ever been to, and I may have missed all of it, if I had not met whoever it was that mentioned that it was worth going to.

If you have ever heard of the Lincoln County War or haven't and just love history, you would love to visit Fort Sumner. All of it is worth seeing and spending some time with.

***

From New Mexico, it was time to head to Arizona. I was going to go see Tombstone with all its history, and get to see one of my best friends from the Marine Corps — my clerk that I had not seen in almost 40 years. This ride ended up being Adventure in every sense that I was looking for it.

The closer that I got to Tucson, home of my friend, the more remote my riding got. And then came the wind, and some chances for CMA service.

I only had a couple hundred miles or so to go to get to Tucson, and the wind was not overpowering yet, but as I stopped for fuel and a break, I met a motorcyclist needing help. His name was Keith, and he had his beautiful Harley loaded in a trailer and headed for New Orleans. He told me that he was on the way to Mardi Gras, and it was clear that without help, his bike would suffer some severe damage along the way.

As we talked and got to know each other, I was able to help get the bike re-positioned and in much better shape for the journey, and I was able to find out about some prayer needs of his. We got a chance to pray before Keith pulled out headed east, as I got ready to get back on the road and head west.

But the delay had cost me. Now the wind was beyond an irritation.

As I rode the remaining mile to Tucson, I got a chance to really work on my prayer life. The warnings of Dust Storms were flashing every couple of miles along the freeway, it seemed, and the small beginnings of storms could be seen in the distance across the desert.

The feeling was not what I had in the snowstorm outside of Albuquerque, but it was similar. There was really nowhere good to stop, but continuing was extremely risky. The wind was blowing not just me, but everything around — and I knew that I couldn't count on things getting better if I delayed.

At least I could see.

The signs all warned that if a severe storm started, I was to "stay in my vehicle," which at least gave me a chuckle. Instead of counting on the signs' directive to keep me safe if things got really bad, I looked for places and made plans of how I would park my bike in a way that I hoped would not get it hit, and then get a hundred yards or so from it, out into the desert, to wait out the storm. Those were contingency plans that I hoped I would not have to execute, and throughout the planning and riding, I prayed.

I finally made it to Tucson and felt like an Adventure Rider, finally, when the clerk at the hotel front desk looked stunned and asked incredulously, "You *rode* through that?!?"

***

The next day, I got to go to a local church and meet some great people. I got to meet a young man working at a service station and connect with him and find out about his life, his time in the military, and his dreams. We prayed and traded contact information, and I was off.

After church, I got to go see the man that I had known as Lance Corporal Reyes, a lifetime ago. I had the chance to do something that is all too rare, and that is tell the truth about what an outstanding Marine Reyes was to the people that mean the most to him, his mother and family. They were visiting from the Philippines, and as we had lunch together, I shared with them how of all the Marines I had ever known, he was one of the top few.

As lunch concluded, and the afternoon got going, it was time for me to head to my final destination of real interest, Tombstone.

I prayed that the wind would not be too bad on the ride, and took off. This would be partly freeway and partly highway riding. Though the wind certainly could have been better, it could have been far worse, too.

I made it to the hotel for the two nights in Tombstone and got ready to soak it all up. I had made it through a couple of days of pretty dangerous riding, and hoped that I was at the end of that type of danger.

***

Tombstone was fantastic! If Dodge City was a 10, Tombstone was a 20. Getting to see the actual spot of the shootout at the OK Corral, walk the actual streets, and learn about all of the history of the place was amazing.

The Bird Cage Theatre still sits as it did when the Cowboys played their last hands of poker there, frozen in time. It's not the Acropolis, the Cowboys were just there in the late 1800s, but for a kid that grew up with the Rifleman and Gunsmoke and Bat Masterson, it was better.

In addition to all of the historical sights I got to see, I also met and prayed and talked about faith with other visitors in various museums and tourist attractions. I don't know that I found anyone who had not heard of Christ, but connecting with people who may have been where I had been when I was unconverted was the real highlight of the trip.

And then, sadly, the sightseeing was over, it was time to head home — and time to check the weather to see what my prayers would consist of as I rode.

The prediction was wind. How bad the wind would be I knew that I wouldn't know until I was in it, but I was exhausted from the trip and ready to get back home, and had no choice but to take my chances.

I took off as early as I could make myself get up, and hoped to get some riding in before the afternoon winds got brutal. I wanted to make it to El Paso for the night. So, I rode despite the danger.

Riding on a relatively lightly traveled roadway with wind is hard enough and dangerous enough, but this was not that. This was riding 75-95 mph on freeways — passing semis and being passed by semis virtually the whole way. With limited roads to get from one spot to another in the lightly populated areas that I was in, I had no realistic option except to ride with all the truckers. And I prayed.

As I rode, on one of those last, dangerously-windy days, I got one of the highlights of the trip that I hope to never forget. If there's one thing that I hate more than riding in severe wind, it's having to corner, while riding in severe wind. Having to calculate the lean angle with the wind is not that hard when riding in a straight line, except for the huge gusts, both natural and from the trucks. When a cornering angle is thrown into the mix, the matter starts to max out the Concern Scale.

I could see the sweeping turn coming and had time to try to work up the math in my head. The angle of the road, the direction of the wind, the gusts, the traffic — it was all banging around in my brain as I rode at high speed and prayed. As I did, and as usual, I had Christian music playing on the headset built into my helmet. Many of the songs on my playlist are old hymns that are my favorites from childhood.

I went into the turn, praying, calculating, and leaning —
praying that the leaning I was doing was correct. And as I did,
the song in my headset changed and on came "Leaning on Jesus,
Leaning on Jesus, Safe and Secure from All Alarms..."

I started laughing.

God showed me His sense of humor as he demonstrated his
protection of me and got me through that turn and the rest of
that day's ride safely. I made it to El Paso, covered in dust, and
closing in on the last part of another great Adventure.

***

I made it home the next day, after a long but relatively uneventful ride. The crazy desert winds were no more, and I only had
to do the normal calculations of how to stay alive on a bike.

Seeing everything I had seen was a dream come true and more
than I had hoped for. A large part of the experience was being
reminded that history isn't always black and white.

Over and over in the history that I saw and read about, I was
reminded that few people are 100% good or 100% bad. Many of
the famous lawmen had been outlaws at one time or another,
and some of the outlaws had been lawmen.

Every bit of that was perfectly in keeping with the message
of the CMA and the Gospel, all of us are sinners in need of
forgiveness, and Christ provides the Way for the reconciliation
with God that we all need.

I have found that reconciliation for myself and I have found my place in the Adventure World.

My Adventures will continue to be a quest to spread the Gospel message to as many people as I can, and doing it as much as possible on two wheels.

EPILOGUE

In Romans 7:15-20, St. Paul wrote, in part:

For I do not understand my own actions. For I do not do what I want, but I do the very thing I hate....For I do not do the good I want, but the evil I do not want is what I keep on doing.

Truer words may never have been written about the Christian Walk. And those words seem so poetically perfect with which to end *Motorcycles and Memories*.

There are so many motorcycle adventures in my mind that I would love to take, yet my bike sits idle so many days – far more than those on which it is ridden.

More importantly, there are so many people that I want to reach for Christ, and yet I sit idle — or worse — day after day.

My sincere hope is that, if nothing else, this book embarrasses me into being less idle in my riding and in my Walk.

See you on the Road.

Thank you to Jocelyn Snow — GS Trophy finalist — for her willingness to help me at a time I truly needed it in my Adventure journey.

Thank you to Jim and Elizabeth Martin — producers of *Adventure Rider Radio* and *ARR Raw* podcasts — for consistently providing inspiration in the Adventure World.

Thank you to Rene Cormier — owner of Renedian Adventures Ltd. — for making me feel welcome in the Adventure World when I first entered it.

And thank you to all those unnamed but not forgotten — the passengers, riders, teachers, fellow Marines, friends, and even strangers who shared the road, offered wisdom, or lent a hand along the way — for helping to make the memories.

ABOUT THE AUTHOR

Eric D. Beal is a lifelong motorcyclist, Marine Corps veteran, attorney, and author who has spent his life seeking both adventure and purpose.

He is the founder of Beal Law Firm, a leading family-law practice in the Dallas–Fort Worth area, and Nocona Injury Law, a personal injury focused firm created specifically to help the people of Montague County. He is Board Certified in Family Law by the Texas Board of Legal Specialization and has been recognized among Texas Super Lawyers and Best Lawyers in America for multiple consecutive years.

Eric's professional life has been defined by the same discipline, integrity, and endurance that guided him as a United States Marine Corps Captain, and those same traits continue to shape his life on two wheels.

An avid adventure rider, snow skier, and scuba diver, Eric has logged thousands of miles across the country in search of open roads and quiet revelations. He and his wife, Sherry, make their home in Nocona, Texas, where the roads are winding, the sunsets are wide, and life still offers new adventures worth chasing.

Motorcycles and Memories: Adventure Beyond the Road is his first book—a reflection on faith, risk, and the freedom found in both redemption and the ride.

ALSO BY

Motorcycles and Memories: Adventure Beyond the Road is Eric D. Beal's first book. He is currently developing additional works that blend personal experience, faith, and hard-earned lessons from the courtroom, the Marine Corps, and beyond. His forthcoming writing will continue to explore leadership, perseverance, and the search for meaning in modern life.